# REZ METAL

Inside the Navajo Nation Heavy Metal Scene

ASHKAN SOLTANI STONE AND NATALE A. ZAPPIA

UNIVERSITY OF NEBRASKA PRESS   LINCOLN

© 2020 by the Board of Regents of
the University of Nebraska

All photos by Ashkan Soltani Stone

All rights reserved

Library of Congress Cataloging-in-Publication Data
Names: Soltani Stone, Ashkan, author.
| Zappia, Natale A., author.
Title: Rez metal: inside the Navajo Nation heavy metal
scene / Ashkan Soltani Stone and Natale A. Zappia.
Description: Lincoln: University of Nebraska Press, 2020.
| This book consists primarily of the voices, lyrics, and
images emerging from Navajo communities and rez
metal culture, and is a companion to the documentary
film Rez metal. | Includes bibliographical references.
Identifiers: LCCN 2019044532
ISBN 9781496205094 (paperback)
ISBN 9781496222480 (epub)
ISBN 9781496222497 (mobi)
ISBN 9781496222503 (pdf)
Subjects: LCSH: Navajo Indians—Music. | Heavy metal
(Music)—Navajo Nation, Arizona, New Mexico & Utah.
Classification: LCC E99.N3 S655 2020
| DDC 781.66089/9726—dc23
LC record available at https://lccn.loc.gov/2019044532

Set in Info by Laura Buis.
Designed by N. Putens.

**Frontispiece:** Kyle Felter with guitar

CONTENTS

List of Illustrations   *vii*

Acknowledgments   *ix*

Introduction: History of the Project and Arrangement of the Book   *1*

1. What Is Rez Metal?   *5*

2. Venues   *43*

3. The Band   *59*

4. Industry, Audience, and the Next Generation   *79*

   Notes   *89*

   Sources and Further Reading   *91*

## ILLUSTRATIONS

Kyle Felter with guitar   *frontispiece*
1. I Don't Konform in Copenhagen   *xii*
2. Lyrics by I Don't Konform   *15*
3. Russell Begaye and Jonathan Nez, Navajo Nation presidents   *16*
4. Jonathan Nez, Flemming Rasmussen, and Russell Begaye   *17*
5. Jerold Cecil of Bourbon Entertainment, manager of I Don't Konform   *19*
6. Edmund Yazzie, member of Navajo Council and Testify   *23*
7. Mechelle Morgan Flowers, Native American teen music program   *26*
8. Lavina Pete, medicine woman   *27*
9. Jay Cee, deejay at Gallup KXX Radio   *30*
10. Country Alibi   *34*
11. Hemlock, at Window Rock   *39*
12. Juggernaut venue   *44*
13. Ernie Santiago, owner of Juggernaut club   *45*
14. Brandon Tsosie, owner of Studio 18   *49*
15. Rez house concert   *51*

16. Rez house concert   *51*
17. Rez house concert   *52*
18. Grandma concert   *54*
19. Grandma concert   *54*
20. Grandma concert   *55*
21. Grandma concert   *55*
22. Grandma concert sign   *57*
23. Testify   *58*
24. Testify   *58*
25. Testify   *60*
26. I Don't Konform   *65*
27. I Don't Konform   *66*
28. Signal 99   *68*
29. Signal 99   *68*
30. Signal 99   *69*
31. Rez Metal house parties   *75*
32. Rez Metal house parties   *76*
33. Melanie Nez   *78*
34. Condemn the World   *81*
35. Kimberly Berchman   *82*
36. Jeff Lee   *84*
37. Teen workshop, Native American Music Fund   *86*
38. Teen workshop, Native American Music Fund   *86*
39. Teen workshop, Native American Music Fund   *87*
40. Teen workshop, Native American Music Fund   *87*

ACKNOWLEDGMENTS

This book rests upon the energy, passion, and creativity of all of the Indigenous musicians featured in the following pages. We are both deeply grateful for the opportunities to meet these people and document this remarkable music scene. We would like to thank the Office of the President and Vice President on the Navajo Nation, Mechelle Morgan Flowers, Craig Matarrese, Veronica Quam (Laydi Rayne), City of Window Rock, City of Gallup, Sweet Silence Studio, SER Studio, Liza Black, Raedean Silversmith-Yazzie, Tito Hoover, Navajo Metal Promotions, Kimberly Berchman, Sammy Chioda, Christopher S. Pineo, Chuck Billy, and the band Testament.

We would like to dedicate this book in loving memory of Edwin Yazzi, Shauna Lee, Reese Tsosie, and other members of the Rez Metal family whom we met and tragically lost during the making of the documentary and this book.

We also thank our editor Matt Bokovoy from the University of Nebraska Press (UNP) for his vision, enthusiasm, and excellent feedback during the process. Thanks as well to Heather Stauffer at UNP and to the anonymous reviewers who helped make this a better book. All the proceeds from *Rez Metal* will go the Native American Music Fund, located in Window Rock, Arizona.

REZ

# METAL

**1.** I Don't Konform in Copenhagen

# Introduction

HISTORY OF THE PROJECT AND ARRANGEMENT OF THE BOOK

This book consists primarily of the voices, lyrics, and images emerging from Navajo communities and rez metal culture. It is part of a larger film project documenting the scene and serves as a companion to the documentary *Rez Metal*. The film, directed and produced by co-author Ashkan Soltani Stone, provides an intimate portrait of the kaleidoscope of musical performances, concerts, and interviews involving its participants. Among the primary filming locations are Window Rock, Thoreau, Ship Rock, and Red Valley on the Navajo Reservation as well as Gallup and Farmington, New Mexico. Soltani further explores different types of venues including the area's central metal venue, Juggernaut music in Gallup, as well as unconventional makeshift spaces on family plots and housing projects. He also films several reservation-based record producers and other Navajo-directed endeavors, including youth heavy metal workshops, teaching programs (sponsored by the Native American Music Fund), and tribal government–sponsored initiatives supporting mentoring for the next generation of rez metal musicians. The film features diverse groups of musicians: from an all-female Navajo metal band to a rez band on the verge of breaking into the mainstream. Most recently Flemming Rasmussen agreed to produce the debut album of I Don't Konform, one of the central bands featured in the film. Mr. Rasmussen has actively participated in the documentary, playing a role as an important character while also hosting I Don't Konform at his Sweet Silence Studios in Denmark. Many of these characters and venues also play a central role in this book.

*Rez Metal* is divided into four sections that include a montage of images and featured interviews. Our first series of interviews follows this introduction in chapter 1, "What Is Rez Metal?" Our interviewees trace its origins on the Navajo Reservation, where it has been the most vibrant and diffuse, discussing the benefits of rez metal but also some of the controversies it has engendered. Among interviews transcribed in this chapter are conversations with Jonathan Nez, who was the tribal president at the time of writing (vice president at the time of the interview), medicine woman Lavina Pete, and Jerold Cecil, manager of I Don't Konform.

Chapter 2, "Venues," focuses on three primary performance spaces for rez metal: Gallup, house parties, and "rez slaughter" tours. We begin at the rez metal mecca of Gallup, New Mexico. Gallup is known as the "capital of Indian Country." With its proximity to several reservations and its service as a destination for major powwows, rodeos, and other cultural events, Gallup proudly celebrates its Native and western heritage. However, darker, more foreboding sides of the city also lurk alongside these events. High unemployment, drug addiction, and a growing homeless population shape the cultural contours of this urban space. Rez metal taps into these tensions, making Gallup a "go to" site for touring bands and hosting a thriving music scene.

The overwhelming majority of fans hail from the Navajo, Zuni, and Hopi Reservations. This chapter explores these unique dimensions through a series of interviews with Ernie Santiago and Brandon Tsosie, owners of the clubs Juggernaut and Studio 18. The section on house parties highlights the incredibly rich and dynamic nature of rez metal. It is at the impromptu jam sessions held at house parties across the reservation that the remarkable sounds emerge. These moments are captured in this chapter through interviews with local bands and fans participating in this shared experience. These gatherings, at times spontaneous, have given rise to more formal, reservation-wide concerts, and description of the "reservation slaughter tour" documents this phenomenon through interviews with traveling bands and fans who all share their deep connections with heavy metal.

Chapter 3, "The Band," closely follows the story of I Don't Konform. This fascinating profile incorporates all of the aspects of the rez metal scene through the journey of the band from the Navajo Reservation all the way to Copenhagen. In the interviews, lead singer Kyle Felter remarks how the band members see themselves as "ambassadors of a nation." This sentiment reflects the transcendent nature of this underground music scene and its ability to make global connections. Other interviewees include Flemming Rasmussen and his recollection of a remarkable trip to meet the band and the Navajo Nation's president and vice president.

Chapter 4, "Industry, Audience, and the Next Generation," presents interviews with band promoters, managers, deejays, and nonprofits involved in utilizing rez metal for education and empowerment across the reservation. Interviews with Kimberly Berchman of Navajo Metal Productions and Melanie Nez (a young metal protégé mentored by I Don't Konform) capture this story. Thanks to the flourishing rez metal scene, a whole new generation of youth is learning how to play instruments and using these skills to create meaning in their lives. It is here, perhaps, that the power of rez metal is the most profound and far reaching.

# 1  What Is Rez Metal?

> ■ Metal is the best kept secret on the Navajo Reservation. The best kept secret in America is [our] underground metal scene.
> —JEROLD CECIL, I Don't Konform

At the end of Gallup's sleepy business loop off New Mexico's I-40 sits one of the epicenters of a very loud and cacophonous music revolution. Remaining somewhat of a frontier outpost on the edge of Indian Country, Gallup has seen better times since its heyday as the backdrop of innumerable Hollywood westerns.[1] In more recent decades, Gallup also experienced the uglier side of the modern frontier in 1979 when its Puerco River flooded through town, unleashing ninety-four million gallons of water contaminated with nuclear waste from the nearby United Nuclear Mine in Church Rock.[2] But Gallup is also a mecca of sorts, drawing international crowds for one of the largest powwows in the world—the Gallup Inter-tribal Indian Ceremonial. Since 1922 the event has featured some of the most prominent dancers and artists from across Indian Country.

Gallup also serves as the center for a raw and exploding heavy metal movement—one that now touches almost every corner of the globe, from Los Angeles to Tokyo and Easter Island to Malta. The all-immersive, dramatic, and even jarring experience of heavy metal has connected the most disparate points on the map—and Gallup is no exception. But perhaps nowhere else has metal captured the ears, rhythm, and hearts of its listeners more than from Gallup's neighbors to the north and west: the Navajo Nation. More bands have emerged from every corner of the reservation (the size of West Virginia, with a population of three hundred thousand) than in any other part of Indian Country—as much as in any other region of the metal music atlas. It is no accident, then, that the annual metal music festival Speckfest is held in Gallup every year, featuring more than twenty bands from the Navajo and Zuni Reservations. And it is no accident that metal luminaries including the producer of Metallica, Flemming Rasmussen, has made the pilgrimage to this corner of Indian Country: this is the place where rez metal began.

Housed at the legendary venue Juggernaut Music, the high-energy Speckfest heats up the otherwise frigid New Mexican air every December. Over the past ten years since its inception, the scene has exploded. A small and incomplete list of bands reflects this musical ecosystem: I Don't Konform, Testify, Flotsam and Jetsam, War Motor, Death Mantra, Sagebrush Rejects, Unsheathe, Shadow Remain, PHX amongst the Dead, Determined, In the Trenches, Poison Insanity, Now or Never, Band of Black, Decapitation of a New Day, The Smylex, and Belletrist.

While it is one of the biggest and most widely known heavy metal music festivals in the region, Speckfest is just one of a seemingly endless array of venues featuring this music in and around the Navajo Reservation. These include weekly events at several spots in border towns, like Gallup, Farmington, and Aztec, but also bigger venues in Albuquerque, Phoenix, and even Los Angeles. In fact, many of the performers at Speckfest hail from LA, making the journey to pay homage to fans coming from around the country. But other venues (featured throughout this book) include more intimate settings: the hogan, sheep ranch, house party, and living room. Appearances in both settings may be meticulously planned (as in the "reservation slaughter tour") or completely impromptu and spur of the moment. They include the "youth" but also tribal councilmen, women, teachers, and elders. Rez metal musicians are sometimes hostile to other "alternative" genres, but more often than not they straddle multiple genres depending on the audience—from hip-hop to reggae to pop, and even to country music, another deeply popular genre on the reservation.[3] At moments captured during Speckfest, we can experience visceral power emanating from the heavy chords, slamming drums, and screaming vocals. The appetite for rez metal, it seems, is insatiable. After two decades in Indian Country, it continues to capture the ethos of several generations and even points to new forms of Indigeneity and what Kristina Jacobsen calls "social citizenship."[4]

*Rez Metal* documents remarkable scenes like Speckfest. As the following pages detail, this venue is just one of many Indigenous spaces where musicians, producers, and audiences tap into the exciting underground heavy metal scene flourishing within and around the Navajo Nation. *Rez Metal* brings you directly to this cultural moment, allowing these participants to tell this fascinating story, relying on their voices, their lyrics, and their spaces to convey the meaning of this music in their day-to-day lives. But ultimately this book conveys so much more than that.

Perhaps more than anything else, the raw and powerful energy expressed by these Indigenous musicians reflects a convergence of history and the future; of tradition and innovation. Rez metal culture is also in some ways Diné culture, played and listened to by multiple generations on and off the reservation. Both men and women participate. Both young and old. In this way heavy metal acts as a cultural glue not unlike other Indigenous cultural and artistic expressions, including other musical genres. The powwow circuit comes to mind, of course, but so do country, hip-hop, and reggae.[5] But *Rez Metal* and its main characters further posit that there is another dimension to this music, a unique, visceral quality of rhythm that channels both the despair and hope—the isolation and sense of community—which makes the experience all the more profound. Before we explore the contours of the rez metal scene, though, we must understand the intersection of music and Indigeneity and ultimately answer the questions: What is rez metal? And *why* rez metal?[6]

**INDIGENOUS RHYTHMS**

When one looks closely enough, Indigenous rhythms, musicians, lyrics, and genres are indeed embedded in every soundtrack of America. Rock, jazz, R&B, country, pop, hip-hop, reggae, punk, electronica—nearly every form of contemporary music has been influenced by Native America. Native instruments have also infiltrated popular music and culture, from the Hawaiian steel guitar to the wooden flute to the leather-bound drum. And even within those genres that are entirely Western, such as classical music, Native practitioners have Indigenized these as well, appropriating and flipping the very symbols of colonialism in all-Indian marching bands, orchestras, and choruses.[7] And then, of course, there are the powwow circuit, Native American flute music, and other forms of traditional music resonating across the Americas. Legions of scholars have explored almost every acoustic angle of Native America, reimagining the soundscape of the Americas but also around the world.[8] As these scholarly revisions accumulate, Native American musicians continue to transgress their status as relegated to being part of the "world music" and "traditional" genres. An increasingly problematic term, world music has come to represent sounds emanating from the developing world (i.e., "non-Western" music). Initially embraced as a way to promote music on the margins, world music has outgrown its status outside the canon and become part of the mainstream.[9]

Exposing the false dichotomy between "traditional" and "modern" expressions of culture not only cuts across Indigenous music but resonates in Native literature, painting, sculpture, and film—all of the arts, in fact. Indeed, the delicate dance between Native expression, cultural appropriation, and art production for outsiders (aka tourist art) has shaped the artistic and historical landscape of both Natives and non-Natives since their earliest encounters. Art in all its forms has increasingly become commoditized, professionalized, and commercialized throughout the twentieth and early twenty-first centuries. For Native artists, their work has also taken on particular forms of political resistance, battling colonialism, overcoming historical trauma, and advancing sovereignty-building projects while also embracing innovative forms and techniques.[10] The contemporary Indigenous art scene has culminated in centers like Santa Fe, where the Institute of American Indian Art continues to showcase generations of Native artists, but also in every artistic capital across the Americas.[11] In similar ways Indigenous foodways and chefs have also made inroads into the larger culinary scene, raising the profile of Native ingredients and traditional ecological knowledge while synthesizing both traditional and Western culinary practices.[12]

While each form of Indigenous expression is distinct, reflecting regional differences unique to each of the hundreds of nations of Native North America (i.e., Navajo, Comanche, Acoma, etc.), there are common threads that shape traditional and contemporary art. These include resistance to colonialism, reservation life, the urban diaspora, Indian Reorganization Act, the Termination Era, American Indian Movement, and the Self-Determination Period. The best examples of these forms of art unite individual artistic skill, community voices, and historical experiences that capture the imagination of both Natives and non-Natives. Again, Indigenous music also provides a lens into these cultural and artistic landscapes. Whether it be the pioneering work of the Indian Reservation Orchestra and its conductor Joe Shunatona, or the jazz of Mildred Bailey, the protest and folk music of Buffy Sainte-Marie, the flute of Carlos Nakai, or the beats of A Tribe Called Red—Native music can be found in every corner of our collective soundscape.

### NAVAJO RHYTHMS

Diné history and culture thus intersect many of these themes shaping Indian Country. During the nineteenth century the Diné fiercely resisted the incursion of the U.S. Army (led by Kit Carson), leading to violent standoffs at Canyon de Chelly and ultimately resulting in horrific incarceration at Bosque Redondo. The Long Walk is remembered as the "Navajo Trail of Tears" and still sears the collective memory of the Diné. In the early twentieth century Navajos adjusted to the realities of U.S. hegemony, even thriving through their successful sheep grazing economy. But government intervention during the Depression again disrupted this Navajo livelihood, forcing the mass slaughter of sheep due to overgrazing. This government policy deeply traumatized Navajo communities, as sheep were considered extended kin and were central to their diet, clothing, and livelihood.

During World War II and the Cold War, Navajos continued to feel the overwhelming impacts of federal policies. Navajos most famously played an instrumental role as code talkers in the Pacific theater of World War II. But perhaps more important, Navajo resources and labor fueled the nuclear age during the Cold War. Situated upon the energy-rich Colorado Plateau, Navajo towns and other communities of the Four Corners region—including the Acoma, Hopi, and Laguna Pueblos and the towns of Grants, Moab, Gallup, and

Durango—particularly experienced the convulsions of Cold War energy exploration and development.[13] Almost every aspect of the nuclear fuel cycle—including mining, milling, enrichment, transportation, and storage—occurred here. As a result of these new energy economies, local Navajo livelihoods shifted dramatically from sheep herding to wage earning.[14] The energy booms (uranium, coal, and oil) during the Cold War provided a brief respite from some of the economic hardships experienced on the Navajo Reservation, and tribal presidents like Peter MacDonald pushed for the establishment of the Council of Energy Rich Tribes (CERT) to protect Indigenous resources.[15] Alongside new jobs, leases increased tribal revenue. By 1978 the Navajo tribe leased more than seven hundred thousand acres of their land to several mining companies.[16] By the 1970s, though, this partnership between the Navajo Nation, private companies, regional governments, and state and federal regulatory agencies had firmly established a pro-energy development culture that in many ways precipitated the worst nuclear accident in U.S. history.

In 1979 a potentially catastrophic accident at the Three Mile Island nuclear reactor plant gripped the U.S. and the world.[17] A nightmare "China Syndrome" was averted, but the near meltdown gave the nation pause. In an unprecedented and dramatic fashion, Americans turned their back on nuclear energy. During the same year and two thousand miles away, Native Americans witnessed an even more devastating nuclear accident on the Puerco River. Navajos affected by the accident also attempted to turn their back on nuclear power. But unlike for most mainstream Americans, Navajos did not have this option. Nuclear waste remained all around them—in the air, water, and land.

The disaster at Church Rock produced profound economic, environmental, and cultural impacts on the Navajos and other southwestern inhabitants, state and federal governments, and the physical landscape of the region. While the spill and the reaction to it illustrated an enduring dependency on the nuclear industry, they also showcased a crucial turning point in Navajo attitudes toward energy development. Unable to rely on their tribal leaders, state representatives, or government regulatory agencies to look out for them, local Navajo communities have begun initiating tighter air and water monitoring projects to assess the amount of radiation in their communities. Through local groups like the Eastern Navajo Dine Against Uranium Mining (ENDAUM), community-based approaches have empowered Navajos to stave off advances made by other mining companies looking to reopen operations in Indian Country. Twenty-five years later, these organizations continue to use the Church Rock spill as their lighting rod to galvanize opposition to future mining.[18]

This long history of entanglements between Navajos and outsiders—encroaching colonial and global forces intersecting local resistance, accommodation, and autonomy—powerfully resonates wherever you travel in Dinétah. And it is most clearly heard in the rapturous drumbeats and chords of rez metal. Rez metal is but one of several musical genres that have swept across the Navajo Nation and Indian Country. As Kristina Jacobsen's intimate study of contemporary Navajo language and identity reveals, Navajo country music is prominent in the culture of the tribe and, like rez metal, is subversive, resisting the dominant culture and applying its own idiom and themes to mainstream country. Navajo country reclaims rural, western culture and makes it Indian, allowing Navajo musicians and listeners to claim country music as their own. Similarly, Navajo hip-hop (and Indigenous hip-hop beyond Dinétah) claims an urban identity and culture seemingly at odds with Indian Country. Like Navajo country, hip-hop appeals to listeners and artists ignored by the mainstream, speaking directly to the frustrations and challenges experienced by Navajos—particularly the younger generations facing widespread unemployment, isolation, and lack of economic opportunities.[19] Hip-hop, perhaps more than country, is seen as "underground" and alternative to mainstream Navajo culture, where country dominates. The rez metal scene, like hip-hop, is seen largely in opposition to traditional Navajo songs and country music.

But the immersive nature of metal puts it within an altogether different musical experience. To experience metal is to get a shock to the system—(more on the history, philosophy, and physicality of heavy metal later)—that provides Navajo bands and their listeners with a cathartic communal experience. Perhaps more than any other genre, rez provides "equipment" to deal with the historical, cultural, and economic trauma shared by Navajos. As the interviewees in this book attest, the music is both an escape from the day-to-day and also a saber to rattle in frustration and anger at the status quo. In contrast to the common perception that heavy metal causes anger and aggression, in this instance, rather, it fosters positive, even nurturing emotions. Rez metal, in fact, creates supportive communities that help people cope with alcoholism, drug abuse, suicide, and unemployment.[20]

**HEAVY METAL RHYTHMS**

As with other "subcultures" expressing alternative music, philosophies, identities, literature, and art, the rez metal scene shares many similar themes and is shaped by the same sociocultural, economic, and historical forces. Heavy metal emerged and evolved from the turbulent countercultural movement of the punk era.[21] Musicologists have identified several overarching sociocultural factors that helped spread heavy metal, pointing to a largely working-class audience located in or near deindustrialized urban areas. Once confined to white (i.e., Anglo or Anglo American) subcultures, heavy metal has transgressed racial, gender, and ethnic divisions.

Now heading into its fifth decade, heavy metal shows no sign of slowing down—a remarkable feat for a genre seen as countercultural or fringe. The music's very durability speaks to both the decentralized nature of metal production (there is no Motown, Nashville, or New York to act as the distribution point) and the universal language inscribed in the metal experience: "*All* metalheads . . . view metal as the opposite of light entertainment. To them, it is a form of serious music that endorses a particular set of values."[22] It is easy to see how these values espousing musical purity with its promise of an unadulterated, unfiltered, and multisensory experience appeal to disaffected and marginalized generations of youth. In the interviews and lyrics appearing in *Rez Metal*, these sentiments reappear over and over again—a need to experience clarity, to connect to a larger moment or purpose, and simply to feel alive and in the moment.

Rez metal achieves this but also tackles particular Indigenous themes through its lyrics and community-based networks of support. Indeed, rez metal provides innovative and enduring networks of kinship that transcend generations (rez metalheads and bands can be found between the ages of ten and sixty), gender (men and women form bands—sometimes together), and class (tribal council members, elders, and high school teachers all are confessed rez metalheads). The spirit is largely cooperative rather than competitive and can be felt in the nodding heads during shows and in between sets as fans share stories, talk about new bands and venues, and revel in their musical comradery. This is the unique spirit that Flemming Rasmussen, producer of Metallica, admired when he arrived on the reservation to hear the band I Don't Konform play in their hogan near Window Rock: "The raw emotion and the thematic rage running through their music [was] something refreshing and unique."

**2.** Lyrics by I Don't Konform

## Jonathan Nez

Today we are having the Office of the President and Vice President's "Hope Fest" here [at Window Rock]. All the metal bands come in from throughout the Navajo Nation, and we're having our own little gathering with all the metalheads. Isn't that something to see and hear? With metal, we want to reinstill hope back into our people. We have a problem within the Navajo Nation about suicide. It is rampant throughout our nation. We're talking about this issue to our folks here. What better way to address this than with all genres of music? We had the "Hope Tent" open to Christian bands on Thursday night. Tonight is for the metal fans. We just want to let people know—not to give up on their dreams, their aspirations. Not to give up on whatever they want to do in their life, especially to the young people out here. Life is precious.

**3.** Russell Begaye, former Navajo Nation president (*left*); Jonathan Nez, Navajo Nation president 2019 (*right*)

What we want to reinstill in our people is that sense of the history of resilience here on the Navajo Nation. We came through some tough times here on the reservation. Starting 150 years ago with the Long Walk. But we came home. Back to our homeland. We're a resilient nation. We're resilient people. Our people are strong. Our people are awesome. What better way to celebrate this than to bring a lot of folks together and just enjoy some great metal music here at Window Rock!

We have some great metal fans here on the Navajo Nation. Metal still lives here. With our talent here on the reservation, somebody is going to break through. Rather than being the opening act, they will be the headliner. I guarantee you that. Sometime in the future we'll get some great talent here on the Navajo Nation. We are at the same time putting hope back into our nation and that's an awesome thing

**4.** Jonathan Nez, Navajo Nation vice president (*right*), Flemming Rasmussen (*center*), and Russell Begaye

to be a part of because there's a movement happening here. People are saying, "Yes we can. We can overcome some tough times and we help each other." We can help our people out there—our elders and veterans. With this event that's happening here we're bringing families together. You've got the younger generation that's going to continue metal moving forward. And it's great to see these young people here with their parents. Some of us grew up with metal back in the day and now the second generation of metalheads are here today. So it's great to be part of it and not just metal. But all genres. We've got country. We had a Christian band, Newsboys, that came out to play. I mean we're trying to cover all the angles here for our people to enjoy. I think it's refreshing. A lot of these bands and people come out from all over the place and it's great to see. Our folks coming together and that's what we want to do. I think that's the biggest goal that we want to see is to have families come together, enjoy themselves, enjoy the music as if this is a family.

You know I grew up with heavy metal. In my younger days I recall some of those great music icons of the day, you know? And now they call it classic rock or classic metal. But back in the day it was great. Back then it wasn't more "family oriented," it was more a message in the lyrics that were a little bit extreme. But with what the band Testify is doing, having a positive message come from that—it's great to be a part of that, and not just for young people but for families to come out and watch the shows. Our show at the Office of the President parking lot there by Memorial Park in Window Rock was family oriented. I saw families—moms and dads my age—they probably grew up with metal themselves. But to come and share that with the younger generation, I thought that was awesome. The concert was over at 10:00 p.m. Everybody went home peacefully. There was no alcohol or drugs, nothing like that. It was really family centered. And you know for me I thought that was the biggest plus of a heavy metal show like that, especially on the Navajo Nation. And that was why President Russell Begaye and myself supported the event and it was great. I had a chance to mingle with some of the young people as an elected official. One of the highest elected officials at one of their concerts. They felt like they were included in government, they were included in politics, even if it's just that one day. I had a great time—a little sore on my neck the next day from headbanging, but it was it was well worth it!

## Jerold Cecil

■ "Without a doubt the most popular music among the youth is heavy metal."

I'm the owner/operator of House of Bourbon entertainment. Today we are in Fort Defiance, Arizona, and apparently we've taken over a

**5.** Jerold Cecil, owner of Bourbon Entertainment and manager of I Don't Konform

house as it seems like it's going to be a pretty good show. There's a wide variety here. There's a death metal band that's just about to wrap up. We have some thrash metal, some speed metal. Without a doubt the most popular music among the youth is heavy metal. You see it everywhere. That's why there's so many people wearing band shirts. You can't go, you can't walk fifteen feet without seeing somebody in a Slayer, Pantera, or hell even a Beatles T-shirt. I think there's something about them in the middle. There's something about metal music that really resonates with the youth. I think it's the rebellious nature of it, definitely the guitar, drum driven. And for the most part, these kids around here, that's pretty much all they have.

There's a myriad of issues on the reservation, the socioeconomic issues, there's issues with substance abuse, issues with kids finishing high school. Heavy metal music helps them to cope a lot with a lot of these unnecessary stresses. And without a doubt, there is a connection between our traditional music and contemporary music. I think Native Americans are rich in oral history and oral traditions. It's basically telling stories, relating how somebody is feeling, relating what they're thinking, and that goes a lot with our culture—especially our music.

There are so many obstacles these young musicians face. First of all I think this is more important. There are a lot of values that cater to the music. It's viewed by the community as evil on the fringe of society and we're basically in a proverbial black hole. Not a lot of eyes on reservation music, and for a band who really wants to get out there, they have to travel hundreds of miles to the nearest cities, Phoenix, Albuquerque, even Flagstaff. And that is pretty much our biggest hurdle—getting eyes on this young group. All these young musicians getting eyes on their bands. I think there was a time when there was a huge opposition against this type of music, but you can sort of sense a gradual shift in the mentality toward the music. Some venues are opening up, but still it's not enough. These kids, they spend thousands of dollars. It's amazing they spend that much money on their equipment. They're so talented, and it's unfortunate that for them to get noticed is pretty much an impossibility.

I first came into contact with IDK [I Don't Konform] when I was a student over at Arizona State and Mesa Community College. I graduated in 2005. My first encounter was helping them get zombie paint for a Halloween show. So I knew some makeup artist in the valley and I arranged things, and they got the makeup paint for the Halloween show. And then they were looking for a show: "Hey, I know this guy that does this thing at this pub," and we got him a show. Then Kyle asked me to help be their manager. At the time I was going to school for forensic psychology at Arizona State. I said, "Okay, how much will this interfere with my schooling?" So, you know, I agreed to do it as a weekend project. They started jamming regularly after leaving the valley. Then they picked up a drummer from another band, and he was just that missing puzzle piece that had "line lock" piece like in Tetris that just connects everything and just blows everything out of the water—that's their drummer Randy. And his drumming skill—can't nobody can touch it on the rez.

Randy's been on the metal scene for years and years. He's a little bit older than us and at times it's kind of hard to deal with all the band because we're all separate, but man, getting this trio and their sound tighter has been amazing. Seeing the progression coming from the valley and back to the reservation, this band is something special. My goal for this band is to bring some light on this underground music scene we have on the reservation. Look at the history of rock 'n' roll. All the big trends happen as regional music scenes, like New York in the '70s and '79. You had the New York Dolls, you had the Ramones. In Seattle in 1991 you had Pearl Jam, Sound Garden, and Nirvana. The Bay Area in 1981 you have Metallica, Anthrax, Megadeth. All these big music scenes come and they hit hard, hit fast. And as time tells, twenty years later they're the bands that make it on the music scene. There are the artists that really have staying power.

You can even trace it back to Manchester. Led Zeppelin, Judas Priest, they all came from Manchester. That's why they call it British Steel, which evolved into British heavy metal. The fact that Black Sabbath's Tony Oh came from the steel mills in Manchester in Britain, and that's where that British Steel, that heavy metal sound came from there. I want this to happen with our music scene, our DNA on the ground. All these bands are promoting, and my number one project—my guy—is the ace in the hole. IDK, they're going to bring all these guys home and the entire world onto the reservation. I guarantee in five years every single record label—Warner Brothers, Interscope—they're all going to be looking to the reservation because this is the scene. You have so much talent here on the reservation that needs to get out there. This is the new scene and that's what I want to bring out when I take IDK overseas to record with Metallica's producer. That's going to be Flemming Rasmussen's next Grammy. Their songs are just straight. Hard hitting and to the point. This whole thing we're doing, sure it benefits us, benefits Flemming; it benefits you. More importantly it's going to bring ice onto this product. The best kept secret in the Navajo Reservation. The best kept secret in America is the underground metal scene.

## Ed Yazzie

■ "We're going to keep it alive."

My name is Edmund Yazzie, Navajo Council member. I represent six chapters of the largest Native American tribe in the U.S. We're the size of West Virginia. This is my third term being on the council. It has been very interesting, especially while also being in a metal band—my son's metal band. I remember advocating, and my elders would tell me in Navajo, "Mr. Yazzie is crazy for being in a metal band." To me it was a compliment. My mom and dad are metalheads too. My dad's a pastor and I remember him buying my first record, which was the ACDC platinum black record. And so from there it just took off. And now with the council they know what metal's about and actually a few of our colleagues have been to our gigs. I was really thankful when one council member commented when we were in session. "You know I've been to many, many concerts and what I've seen with Mr. Yazzie's band is just like going to a big concert."

So I play the drums. I started when I was eleven years old. Now I'm forty-seven, so I have a lot of experience. I love it. I love metal. I know music is music, but to me the way I see metal is that it's all about talent. The guitar riffs, the vocals, and especially the drumming part. Now

**6.** Edmund Yazzie, member of Navajo Council and of Testify

there are bands like Lamb of God, where we see the double basing, and Metallica, of course, and Iron Maiden and that type of style. It's all about talent. And that's my passion and I know it's kind of funny. We're supposed to dress up in the "metal." As you could see I don't have any Metallica or Godsmack shirt on. But my heart is metal all the way, and it is just remarkable being in a band, my own son taking the lead and me drumming.

And now there's talent among our Navajo kids. There's bands from Crown Point like Born of Winter. When we play with them the talent is unreal. I'm glad that we're finally going to expose the music industry on the rez because if only the bigger bands knew how our kids are actually playing some of their cover tunes out in the middle of nowhere. It's amazing. We know bands from California, from Japan, going back to the '80s with Judas Priest's Rob Halford. I actually tried to send a letter to Rob Halford. He lives in the Phoenix-Scottsdale area, and I actually tried to get him to play in our fair here in the Navajo Nation.

When our council was in session we would get reports from different departments and I remember in my second term making a statement saying, "You know, instead of bringing the country artists to the annual fair, we need to be exposed to the metal sector." We had our first experience in actually bringing a pretty big metal band to the fair, which was about three years ago. The band was Korn, and my gosh it sold out in our fairgrounds. Arizona police were here. State police. And they thought it was going to be a big old riot. But in reality it was just one good show, and I even went to that concert and had a good time. So that's opening doors. I heard one of the staff who said because of my comment that was made on council, we're expanding the music sector for new artists. I'm fortunate and I'm very thankful that I'm on the council where we could express [this] and bring out the talent among our Native kids. And you never know. Just like Blackfoot. Blackfoot is a Native American band that made it in the rock sector. Our local bands are going to hit the bigger arena. It's getting there. Give it another five, ten years. It just amazes me when we go to Albuquerque or Phoenix and with that we have to drive three hours just to go to a big show. But it's worth it. One day one of our local bands here is going to make it. And so I'm just hoping that that one day will come soon.

Yeah, we have rap. I mean we have country, hip-hop, and reggae also coming out. But I'm also going to be faithful to the metal sector. Why metal music among our people? As a child growing up, when we were always with our moms and dads, grandpas and grandmas, uncles and aunties, you would always hear country being played. When metal came in through the media such as cable or maybe family and friends, we would have a Ted Nugent tape or ACDC record. And that exposed us and later our kids. For me, I was like, "Wow, this music has a different heavy sound." That was before I started playing the drums, and it was just an aggressive beat. Then getting the lyrics, you could relate to relieving a few of your stress makers. This is what's currently going on now. When I get frustrated it usually helps. You know there's a couple of songs that I like when I'm especially frustrated in a council meeting. And those words can help the soul. To me, metal to me is about talent. When we were kids, we had to listen to Hank Williams or Earl Thomas Conley. I'm not putting these artists down. They were just the same type of beat all the way through. But I remember hearing my first record of Ronnie James Dio in high school. I was blown away by that. And then I did more research and learned about Iron Maiden, Rush, and Judas Priest. I actually started going to concerts back then and I remember my first big concert was Judas Priest when they came out with Whitesnake. That was in Albuquerque. I was just so blown away by that. And so now it has grown and grown. We took my son to his first Metallica concert (he's twenty-two years old now) when he was only in third grade in Phoenix.

And it's that type of exposure that's getting our kids to go into metal now. One good concert that we played in was opening for Double Driver, and that was here in Window Rock. The lead singer has always really catered to Native Americans and said that our people have gone through a lot, and it's always an honor for the band to come down and do a set. I remember when Ronnie James Dio passed away. I've got all his records. But I felt an emptiness. You know, it's been sad that he's gone on, but I remember in one of his interviews he stated that "whatever happens, you've got to keep metal alive." I think metal was almost dying out, but not anymore with all the bands that are coming out. That's what I tell my son—we're trying to keep it alive.

The kids that are just starting come up to me and want to learn how to play guitar. We take that seriously. I've done drum lessons

**7.** Mechelle Morgan Flowers, program director for Native American teen music program

with little kids, and now they're buying these massive kits that are probably a lot better than my kit right now. I don't see it's going to die out here. We're going to keep it alive. My daughter is only six years old. I get a little bit frustrated when she wants to listen to Katy Perry, but she knows about Iron Maiden and Metallica, going to school with her first Metallica shirt when she was only in preschool. So if we want to keep that, pass it to our young kids, we can make it happen. Keep it alive.

## Mechelle Morgan Flowers and Lavina Pete

■ "It is able to uplift them and their energy."

MECHELLE FLOWERS. My name is Mechelle Morgan Flowers. I am the program director for the Native American Music Fund for five years now.

**8.** Lavina Pete, medicine woman

LAVINA PETE. My name is Lavina Pete, medicine woman. I was raised on the reservation of the Navajo Nation. I reach out to young children to help them be balanced within their system and work. We are here basically for the youth. We want to help them and guide them and support them in their passion in music with music.

MECHELLE FLOWERS. Music is important to them to be able to identify their talents and their interests in who they are. We identify what works for them and what doesn't work for them, especially at that young age. We help them identify being Native American, raised on a tribal nation, living in poverty, and being able to survive and reach out and touch other people by using music. It works for them, being able to find their talents and reach out to create more income, more learning, We work with them at their heart level, just like native elders look upon their youth to be able to have them make the right choices in life. And it takes time. There's a lot of experiences that they will encounter.

LAVINA PETE. But there's always a family-oriented support in the background. We hope that they make the right choices as they mature and pass that on when bringing up their own family. Native Americans have certain events in the Navajo language, including dancing and music powwows. Native American powwows have been song and dance. They have country music that has Navajo language in it. So it's around us. We were raised around that, and they have Navajo ceremonies and different things like that in Navajo language. But this is unique for the young children or the young people in a sense that they find rock. What is the rock music? What does the high pitch volume do to really get in touch with their heart and their soul? It is able to uplift them and their energy. But also helps them to let go.

You know the elders and the parents of these children were raised to be able to make the right choices, to teach them at a certain level of understanding who they are as Diné. Being raised around the ceremonies and speaking Navajo. To sing and dance in their language. At this time, at this generation, society brings in something unique, which is the rock music, and it touches these youth in themselves to be able to create something unique in them and almost wakes them up to a certain level and understanding that this is a new generation. That's what we're talking about.

If you go on the Indian reservation you'll hear a lot of country music. You know you'll hear all the different types of music that come about. And limited radio stations are around. But rock music kind of throws it off to some point because you don't really understand the language behind it. The voices are really kind of thrown out there. But you hear the volume of that music, everyone watching the instruments playing all at once, and it hits right in the center of their body. They say music and dance uplifts you and creates a sense of comfort to some point. But rock music or music that is really at a high pitch—there's some energy that one can interface and that might emerge to where it's not good, because in a sense you don't understand what the language is behind it.

MECHELLE FLOWERS. But they're really feeling these instruments that are playing all at once and it's vibrating through their body. And being a Navajo, you're working with the four elements. You've got water. Fire. Air. And you've got Mother Earth. We're working with nature. So sometimes when you live a life from the past and your past life experience or something that wasn't good—it's just inside you and then released. Sometimes when they're dancing and when they're listening to this type of music. It's almost like a release of a good feeling. We like our youth to get out there and explore and adventure out and enjoy that. Identify who they are and where they come from. Identify their passion and what they enjoy doing. And this is like an active social activity. And so, in that sense when there's substance abuse or alcohol involved or drugs, it throws everything off. And it just doesn't work. It just [clicks off]. And the behavior goes away and they go too deep into it. And that's where the mishap happens.

But if they're doing this just for a bit of caring for each other and being happy and enjoying each other with the sense of them, everybody likes this. It's an enjoyable event to watch. But it takes time to get used to that hard high pitch volume music playing all at once. One time I had stayed. I had went into an auditorium and I got too close to the speaker. And I had this really crushing moment that just frankly pushed my heart to beat really fast.

**9.** Jay Cee, deejay at Gallup KXX Radio

## Jay Cee

■ "What does metal mean to me? Metal is justice."

My name is Jay Cee, and I work at the classic rock station 93 here in Gallup, New Mexico. And I am from the pueblo Santo Domingo and Hopi tribes, and I meet a lot of bands—classic rock bands also into heavy metal bands—all types of rock and heavy metal. The metal scene here is actually growing and it's crazy. We're in an area not like Los Angeles or Dallas or New York City. But it's just continually growing. Different bands on the reservations even from parts you never heard of. And the main bands are the kids who are growing up with this music. They're actually going after forming their own bands, and they are awesome. This is catching the eyes of actual "top name" brand bands like Slipknot Soil. Just a lot of bands that roll through and they're actually surprised, because the response that they get is more phenomenal than in the bigger cities when they're performing there. And that's awesome, because it's just continually growing. There's always bands coming out.

And when you go and see them these guys are really, really good. I'd say it's much needed and [billowing up around] people. The reason why it's growing so much is because it's kind of like a generation gap. Everybody's just like, "Oh, we're just the angry generation." You know that economy and poverty, the starvation, the drinking—everything—and we need it, we need something like this just to vent everything out, family issues and all kinds of stuff. That's true.

Being a deejay here in Gallop, I and most of my listeners grew up in the '80s, and there's nothing really to do here on the reservation. And so they're venting. I mean these guys are really talented—really. I met some of the bands here and it's just amazing that they're going to make it big and get onto different labels. So why metal? What is what is about metal that's not, say, hip-hop or rock 'n' roll? I mean metal was rock 'n' roll but why now? I would say that with Natives, they like that whole drumming thing. Like it was kind of the oldest instrument in the world, you know, but when it comes to music I think we can relate to the whole structure of heavy metal.

Why heavy metal versus not hip-hop—not reggae, not country? As a deejay, I've worked in all those stations. But I can get into the rock, I can get into the heavy metal. I can't get into country, can't get into hip-hop. I'm not saying that's bad. There are people who can. But here it's just more dominant and you get to let loose a lot more than you can versus country and everything else. You just get it out and it's all cool, just like, you know, muscle cars, apple pie, and baseball. There's so much poverty, there's so much going on—how else can you vent it out? If you listen to some of these bands, the lyrics are about that kind of thing, and they're just getting it out. And when you meet these guys they are like way super cool, really nice guys. They're happy because they get all their aggression out, right? When they're frustrated by something they'll go on stage and just let it out.

The [Gallup club] Juggernaut brought in all kinds of crazy bands like Hemlock, which is really popular among the Natives. They're just one of those bands that you can really relate to. Also El Morro here in Gallup, New Mexico. They sponsor host shows. The scene hasn't been filmed here or anything like that because everybody's focused on LA. So when they do come, it's like "wow!" The music has resonance with people because they identify with it. On the reservation, there's literally nothing to do. You see your relatives start drinking. And it's hard for them to get a job because there's no jobs located on the reservation. So they have to travel to get a job, and they need a good car—it's not that easy. So there's a lot of problems with the reservation. I grew up in Zuni. It's a "small town." Nothing really to do but get in trouble. The music is probably one of the things you can do to express yourself and keep yourself sane. So concerts are very popular because that's the only thing to really do and to really enjoy clean and sober. Sometimes the older generation are seen there. Parents too.

Some elders in Zuni think it's a bad thing because they want us to go to the traditional places. We have duties to do and responsibilities, some dealing with our religious culture. That's all great and something that we need to keep on doing. But I think like the later generation of parents are all for it because it keeps their kids out of trouble and their passions going. But they also like the kids to participate in religious ceremonies and responsibilities to keep the traditions alive. So there is a good thing to it. And then there's also bad things to it. It's still balancing out. Most of my listeners, they do have kids. And so there are some old rockers out there, which is kind of cool because they introduce their kids to music. There's no problem with that at all.

And so I like what I see. I like some of the artists that I talk to — really educated. You'll see them with the long hair and all the tats and everything like that, but these guys are about the coolest people we can meet. And I'd rather have my kids follow people like that versus somebody that's not really doing the right thing. You can't judge a book by its cover. So I'm glad that that the older crowd is still coming out. When we have concerts they still call for requests. So it also educates the younger folks musicwise and expands their knowledge of it.

What does metal mean to me? Metal is justice. I started in Zuni. I got inspired to play music and to take pictures for bands. I thought: "This is this is something worth pursuing," and metal to me helps release all my anger, all my frustration. It's therapeutic when I go to a show I like and I participate in some mosh pit. You just release all kinds of stuff, and once you leave you're just like the happiest person in the world. Metal is getting into my car. Getting on the road. Don't know where I'm going and having that music blasting loud and just enjoying it. Listening to the lyrics. Just being free and just listening to it, just having it — major screaming on it, whatever — just letting loose and not even having any worries about it. And for me that's what it is. Just getting up, the stage is pounding your face. Get your horns up and everything about it. And they're letting it loose. I love metal and that's the only way that I can function.

**10.** Country Alibi

## Country Alibi

■ "A lot of the heavy metal bands were cool with each other."

We started back in 2014. On Veterans Day. We had an event. And I was with the band before the band broke up and we had already booked the date for Veterans Day. I had to get some guys together, so I end up calling Preston Khatar and I had another guy—the original drummer Henton. And then through Preston we got to know our bass player. From there we started, we performed that first show. And right after the show we decided to start a band. We originally started out as A Perfect Alibi. Around Gallup we found out that there was more of a rock blues band already called Perfect Alibi. So from there I decided to call us Country Alibi. It will be three years this coming Veterans Day [since we started] the original band. It's only me and Preston that are left. There's a lot of bands out here. And it's hard to find good players, but Preston's been there from the start. I grew up listening to country. Punk rock and country. But mostly country.

I handle all their calls if somebody has a question. I try to answer them as best as I can, and I make sure that every band member is at every gig where they're supposed to be. I keep them all in line, checking on this mission almost every day.

The most popular music I would say is country and classic rock. Classic country. And there's also another genre around here we like to call wrist bands, which is a lot of the local bands that put up different types of CDs. Some have covers and a lot of them have originals. So that's a big genre around here. It's a mixture. We get a mixture of classic country from Waylon [Jennings] to King George [Strait], Bucho [DeGo], and stuff like that—stuff people grew up with around here. And a lot of heavy metal bands—Teleco, ACDC, Def Leppard, Leonard Skinner. So yes, I enjoy classic rock. Any type of music that's good music is good with me. I don't claim just one genre of music. I listen to all types of music, including contemporary jazz.

My late father, who passed away back in 1999, he played in a band around here. He started a band way back before I was born and [played] until he passed away. He was playing in a band at local bars, local venues, so I grew up listening to that group. I tend to just lean toward it, and a lot of the people here, they like country music. They like to swing, they like to line dance. Heavy metal—you can't really dance or two-step to it so much, and that's [the role of] country music. I mean, I think country music is the most dominating. Yeah. The younger generation are more into the metal music and the elders are more into country. A lot of older folks who come around find the country more soothing and calmer. We kind of blend both—rock with country—so it tends to work out pretty good. They can play a clean country sound but he kicks on his distortion pedal now and he can get some rough music. Nobody's been able to put their music out there in a way that will touch everybody, to reach everybody. I mean, if you look at our country music, not many people can travel to Las Vegas or California to see an actual country superstar. We hear different stories saying that with the country music scene, it's a lot more competitive. If I look to more of the heavy metal bands, they are more together. They support and help one another. A lot of the heavy metal bands were cool with each other. And if you were to go to a country music scene, it's more competitive. That's why a lot of bands tend to break up and go their separate ways.

I love what I do. I love to perform. That's my music. My microphone is my drug. I've never done it for the money. It's more for the joy of playing. And to see the people enjoy it. That was more of a payoff for me than anything, and it still is to this day. My band has become a family to me. They're my brothers. Everybody we've met along the way, all are my brothers. Metal bands look like they're having more fun when they perform. If you go to a metal show, everybody is having a good time from start to finish. It's a good time because they hardly see each other and they break out there for music, and some guys write their own music. So it's pretty good. I've seen a lot of heavy metal shows around here, and those guys kick ass.

But metal is always going to be the stepchild. Because there's bands out there that give it their all and sound pretty good. And then there's other bands out there that are just plain noisy. I mean they don't really give much thinking into their music. They just get on stage, start screaming, turn up their volume and all that. But there's a lot of bands—good bands—after that. They put out good music and I think, "You know, everyone needs to just give each other a shot and work together like a family." And I believe that. We can all be one big music scene down here on our reservation. So many elders are still learning about metal. Others don't like to hear it. But I think it's more about the venue where they're set up. A lot of metal shows around here—they're more like bar scenes or outside a bar, and [some people] don't like to go to places like that. Sometimes their highs are way too high. And their high notes or just screaming kind of pinches your ear a little. And I think that's more or less why a lot of people don't like to listen to heavy metal, because it's too loud.

With metal it's different. We look at not only the music. We look at how they play or what they play or how their sound is altogether. From their vocalist to their bass player to their drummer. We look at everything, so it's different from somebody just coming in from outside. As for country music? I mean, you've got classic country. You've got modern country now. You've got pop country. And pop country is more or less not country. It's popular—but it's not country. I tend to listen more to the '80s to '90s country. Back then they actually had stories. You can listen to a song and really picture the story that the person who wrote the song is telling. And you listen to pop country nowadays—it gets you confused, because you don't know what's being said. We see our music as modern country. It's old country with the new sound. A lot of my songs are recorded [privately, so as to protect them], because it's hard to find a recording studio around here to actually publish and copyright your music. We do tend to try to put life on the rez inside our music.

Alcoholism is pretty big here on the reservation. It's a huge issue. Drug use is becoming a pretty big issue here too. A lot of unemployment. It's really kind of hard to pick just one problem. There are so many right here on the reservation. But I think alcoholism is one of the tops. I lost my father to alcoholism. He drank himself [into] alcohol poisoning. Preston's late brother died in a car accident due to a DWI. And my wife, Frager, our manager, she's lost her brother to alcoholism. So you know that's deep [in our lives]. We play a lot of venues like bars, local bars and casinos that serve alcohol. But none of my guys in my band drinks. I've been sober five years. Preston's never drunk, and our best player doesn't drink, and our drummer doesn't drink. We're sober here. That's gotten us a lot of good feedback from a couple of venues. We'll see some bands who by their second set are totally trashed and they're ruining their music on stage. That's been the downfall for a lot of musicians around here.

I grew up around here and I've seen a lot of musicians go down because of alcohol. So what is the biggest misconception about country music? Well, I believe a stereotype is if you like country then you're drunk—"you like to go to bars, you'd like to dance," we say around here. You like to pick up different women whenever you go out, you know. Everybody from here knows there's ladies night Wednesday night. If you're a country fan, of course you're going to be there. What else that's different from metal? Well, a lot of rodeo fans are country music fans. That's another big thing around here on the reservation, rodeos. People tend to go to rodeos. Cowboys and cowgirls like country music. You could play at a fair where there's a rodeo that's been going on, and you get a pretty good crowd from the rodeo. And they're usually pretty calm too, as it were. You play at a bar here in town—let's say Fourth of July weekend—and you get everybody just coming out to have a good time. And you know how that goes. It tends to get a little rowdy. And you know us as a band, we get rowdy ourselves. They feed off everything they get. The crowd is very energetic. They get that energetic vibe. They get into their music. They go into their own world. They forget about the surroundings, the people around them. They just listen to the music. They just start dancing themselves.

**11.** Hemlock, at Window Rock

## Hemlock

■ "They like it because it's raw and it's pure and it's not bullshit."

What's up, everybody. We are Hemlock from Las Vegas, Nevada. But technically now we're from the world because we travel everywhere, always on the road from heaven. Gallup, New Mexico, is one of our favorite places in the world to play because there are lots of rock 'n' roller and metalheads here. It's always fun. I mean, a lot of them are Navajo but we also play down in Zuni and then there are some that are Pueblo. There's some Laguna folks out there too. We do really good out this way. We were one of the first out of town touring bands to play on the rez as far as I know; probably almost twenty years ago now we were invited to play in Tuba City, Arizona. It's like the heartland of the Navajo Nation right there. So we came from Las Vegas, Nevada, and we did a metal fest—it was one of the first ones that I know of—and played in Tuba City and we made a bunch of friends and a bunch of fans and family all at the same time.

There were probably three or four other bands back in the day. There was another kind of wave of Native American bands that were awesome. There's a bunch of good bands from the Flagstaff area and then even up in Shiprock—we've played a bunch of farming tents like on the border up there. We played Tuba City fair one year and then actually our last tour we rolled through in July and we played in Window Rock, Arizona, up there at the president's parking lot right in front of the Window Rock. It was epic. The weather was beautiful. The rock was the backdrop, the rocks and the wind. When we do the big metal fests up in Albuquerque—we played up there with Slayer and Marilyn Manson—you can look out over the audience and I'd say half of them are Native. They love metal Slayer or Metallica or Testament. They like it because it's raw and it's pure and it's not bullshit. It just is the truth and it cuts through and it's heavy.

Yeah, it's not like a product, it's not like the labels and the marketing and this and that, just putting out this same thing over and over again. It's true, like a good pure form. It helps them to cope with their everyday life. I think it helps any person. You know music is an outlet art. It's just a creative outlet. So [sometimes] I'll grab a band from the rez and have them go out of town with us on tour so they can see more places and go out and do more shows, you know. But I think the music also just kind of brings the underground together, and it brings all of the youth together. You are the outcasts of society, and the music is what bonds them together and makes it the collective. So it probably has some of the same stuff with Native Americans. But that is not a passing fad either. It's heavy. But we've been playing on the reservations for over twenty years now, and we keep coming back year after year after year, and we've made some of the best friends ever. They're definitely the most energetic crowds. They're just so energetic.

I'm so happy that we're here. We want to thank everybody for the support over all the years. We're going to keep coming back and coming back. We've rocked the Balmoral theater quite a few times. We've played in towns that most people don't even know are there. We've played in Chinle and we've played in Kayenta quite a few times. I mean we've got friends all over and it's cool. So the music's definitely the glue in the bond among everybody, for sure.

# 2 Venues

> ■ Country sings heartbreak their way, we sing our heartbreak this way.
> —BRANDON TSOSIE, Paranormal

Heavy metal thrives in seemingly lifeless, usually industrial spaces—neglected storefronts, parking lots, construction sites, and windowless dives. Rez metal has reached into similar spaces along the borders of Indian Country, particularly in places like Gallup and Farmington. But Navajos have also carved out unique performance spaces within Indian Country. The traditional hogan and sheep ranch have served as frequent settings. So too have trailers, government housing, and natural landscapes that dominate the reservation. These uniquely Navajo spaces not only enhance the acoustic experience but also allow participants and audiences to reaffirm and reimagine Native sounds, places, and cultures.

Venues, then, are not simply the backdrop. They serve as active participants that shape and reenergize rez metal, facilitating the creation of almost sacred, timeless moments. These venues likewise serve as stops on home-grown rez metal tours, such as the "slaughter tour." Rez metal also reaches outside of the confines of the reservation. In fact, the border acts as a cultural meeting place where bands from all over the region meet and share ideas, rhythms, and styles, pushing new forms of metal into existence. At places like the Juggernaut, Indigenous

**12.** Juggernaut venue

and non-Native metal thrive. In the voices of Diné youth and spaces like "Grandma's concert" and "Rez house concert," we experience the primacy of place in the rez metal scene.

## Ernie Santiago

■ "Everybody loves to mosh here. It's pretty intense."

My name is Ernie Santiago. I am co-owner and operator of Juggernaut Music here in Gallup, New Mexico. We are surrounded. We're kind of like a hope to the reservation—the Navajo Reservation, the Zuni Reservation—and there's a lot of music in this area. There's a lot of metal music; there's different genres. I would say metal is the most popular. Our mission here is basically to help these bands get out there. I mean we do shows, we do live shows. We now have a music star, as you can see. And over here we are in the process of doing a

**13.** Ernie Santiago, owner of Juggernaut club

recording studio, actually, and we are a team. You know, we're like a lot of people who make this happen, and I'm just one guy, one of the co-founders of this whole operation and that's just so we do things all together for the love of the music.

It's a good place. It's nice. You can see all of this is under renovation. There's a lot of construction going on. There's always something that's being worked on, something that we're developing and just growing. Now we're going into a recording studio. The other corner of the operation is Jude. He's going to be heading up a bunch of the producing and everything. He went to school for it, and it's his passion. We're going to focus on [a range of genres]. I'm pretty sure the majority of what's going to come in is going to be a lot of metal, a lot of rock, and hip-hop seems to be pretty popular. I'm a supporter of basically everything out there, and we don't discriminate. Hey, there's a lot of country acts around here, [serving] the older crowd who like to drink. We're not opposed to helping anybody.

From 2009 to 2012 the Juggernaut had a very good run. We hosted over 250 shows. I would say the majority being metal rock. Everybody is so excited in energy, you know, and we try to provide a good show. Everybody loves to mosh here. It's pretty intense.

It's good to be in a position where I'm responsible enough to maintain my life and be able to put out more for people—the younger people, the older people—just give them a little bit of opportunity. Yeah, it's just fun. I would say it has a small town feel, definitely on the up and up, and there's only so much room for growth here in Gallup, because it's really small and it's surrounded by the reservation, of course. So I think it's not going to grow physically but it's going to grow more in the sense of the culture, the younger generation getting older and exploring new options and doing new things. That's why we're here with this. We feel that we're part of that generation and we're able to give back as well as do what we like to do and be happy with what we do.

Metal is a lifestyle. Metal is the way you view things, looking at things from a certain perspective. And having a certain edge and living your life that way. I mean it's really easy to let go and just go out of control with metal. So most people who can't perceive it right think that metal is just chaos and that there's no message in it. To me, metal is a lot more than that. It's just basically grabbing life by the balls and living in it no matter what it is. And I think when people play music, they release a lot of that energy, that stress, into it.

I think metal is angry music, you know, but it's bringing the message across. And in a good way. You know it varies from band to band. Metal is metal is basically a way of life. I guess you can say most people who play metal don't live, like, perfect lives. You know they go through struggles. They go through all kinds of stuff. Metal is a struggle. You know what I'm asking is: Do you think this has something to do with the popularity of heavy metal among kids, even younger generations? Is this something to do with that? Why do you think so? Why not? New music, and it's weird because you know I mess around in different genres, and I find in hip-hop you can express a lot more verbally, but not everybody has that gift around here. And a lot of people have the gift of sound, and they're able to play. I think it's so popular because people are able to release their feelings like that without having to speak, or without having to really explain themselves too much; you know, they can just play what they feel. A group of people can play what they feel, whether it's angry or whether it's a B, or whether it's sad. I just think a lot of people can relate to that.

The subject matter of the songs is something that varies, but I would say the majority of it here in this area is a lot about who you are, about your culture, self-respect, respect for the brothers and for the sisters. A lot of people here are self-reliant, a lot of people work for themselves. They don't want to go out and get a job and punch a clock 9:00 to 5:00. Some groups address political issues, water conservation, and a lot of the way that some of the government has issues with the Navajo Nation. There's a lot of bands that stick up politically. I would say there are some groups that [focus on] heartfelt stuff like suicide. I mean it can get deep—it just depends on the group. Most definitely I think it helps the people who listen to it.

There's not much money in it for any bands around here. I hate to say it, but you make more money playing country at the casinos. A good middle-range group can't even get into a casino because they discriminate. They don't understand the music. So it can be tough just to have a place to play. I'm pretty sure that's how they feel. And that's how I feel. I try to pay bands whenever we can. If we have a local band open up for a bigger band, and they have to travel from Arizona or Fort Defiance, we kick in some gas money. It's really hard to get metal bands paid in this area. Everybody pretty much does it for the love. I'm in a band, and we don't get paid to play, and we love to play. We play every opportunity we can. Anytime somebody asks us to play, we go for it. Being in a band is quite an experience. And you just pretty much got to go for it and not expect to get too much out of it financially.

People throw together shindigs here and there—house parties and stuff. And I think that's what kept everything going when the venue was closed. We also had a couple of small art galleries in town, and we kept the scene alive. So yes, it's not just one dude or this guy. It's a group of people who do what they've got to do to make it happen.

## Brandon Tsosie

■ "You will find peace of mind through metal."

This is where we live. That's our Studio 18 where we put on shows. It all started with the band—my band—Paranormal. After that we started bringing more bands out from the rez, going house to house. All the bands play different genres, not specifically metal. They go black metal, death metal, common, heavy metal, metalcore, and so on. It all helps calm yourself, helps find your peace of mind in metal. I look at it that way: you will find peace of mind through metal. We've been doing this for about six years now. We never had any complaint from anybody, which is great. I think the biggest draw we got is from the band Signal 99. They always really energized things up. They play industrial. [They've] been around for a good decade now.

I would say it's a win or lose situation around here. We have a lot of venues that got closed down, or shut down because of liquor

**14.** Brandon Tsosie (*right*), owner of Studio 18

licenses or stuff like that. So far we still have an entertainment team, which is run by Brian Johnson.

We're doing our own thing up here. Mostly underground stuff. It rests on the underground. Most bands don't have anybody that helps produce them. All these bands that are local are considered underground. They all write their own music individually. Most don't have a producer, although some eventually get one. But they all need someplace to go to imitate metal bands. And this is what we've tried to [supply]. We're a drug-free, alcohol-free event for all ages. And a lot of parents get involved with this—the ones who aren't hardcore Christians (some [band members] rebel against their parents with metal).

I think most everybody likes metal, and it's not against their religion just because they like it. It's their peace of mind that they find with metal. Some parents out there have made up their mind that heavy metal is devil-worshipping music—which it's not. Country sings heartbreak their way, we sing our heartbreak this way. Where I stand, I really love this music. I have a passion for it. I guess what it's done is brought me to this point, to where I am now, and I'm thankful to have music in my life. As I said, I've done this for six years. It's been a rough road, but you know it just keeps me going every day to look forward to something in the evening or to get in contact with bands that are from all over the United States, stuff like that. It's really awesome.

And it's like, wow, there's all these Navajo bands out there and nobody knows who they are. They're just as good as national bands. Even better. People probably think that Native Americans are just mostly remote Indigenous people. We're trying to get ourselves [heard], trying to say that we're here, and we do everything that everybody else does. We're all in the same boat. So bands playing at Studio 18 turn it into a jam session where they can, like, exchange ideas. So they kind of support each other. That's what Studio 18 is about.

**15 & 16.** Rez house concert

**17.** Rez house concert

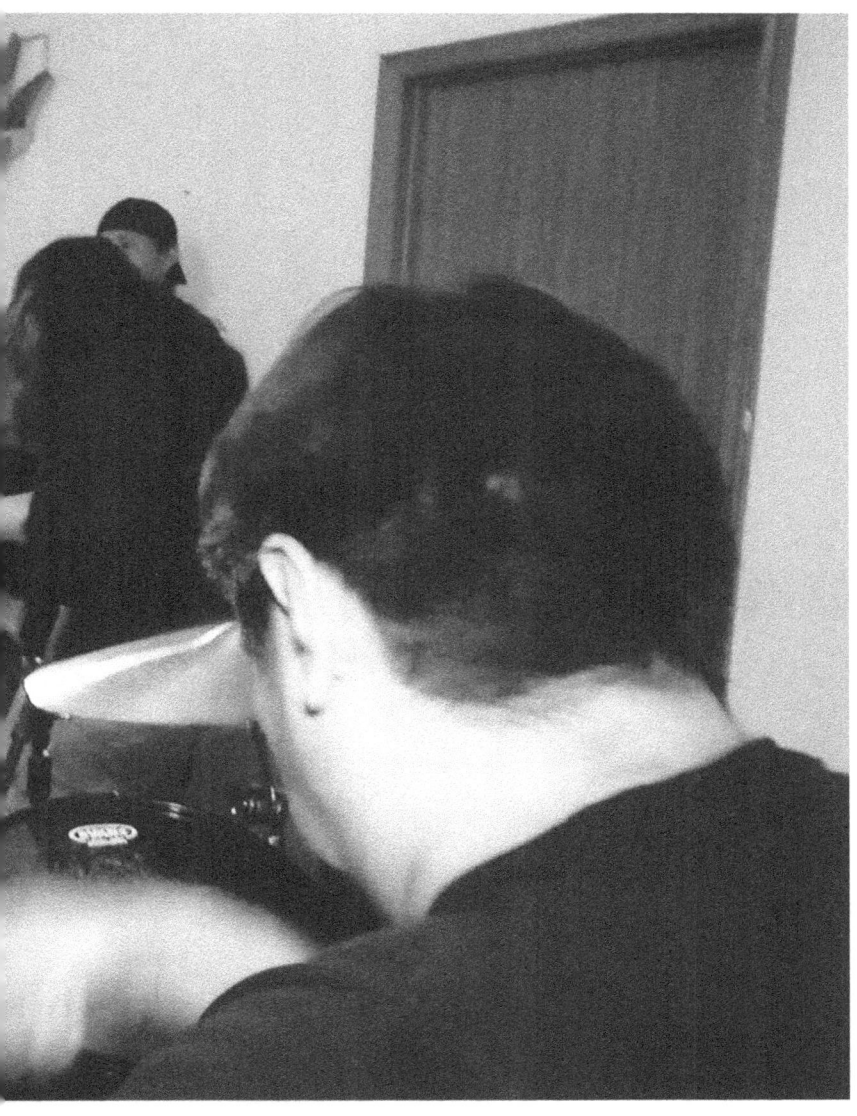

**18–21.** Grandma concert

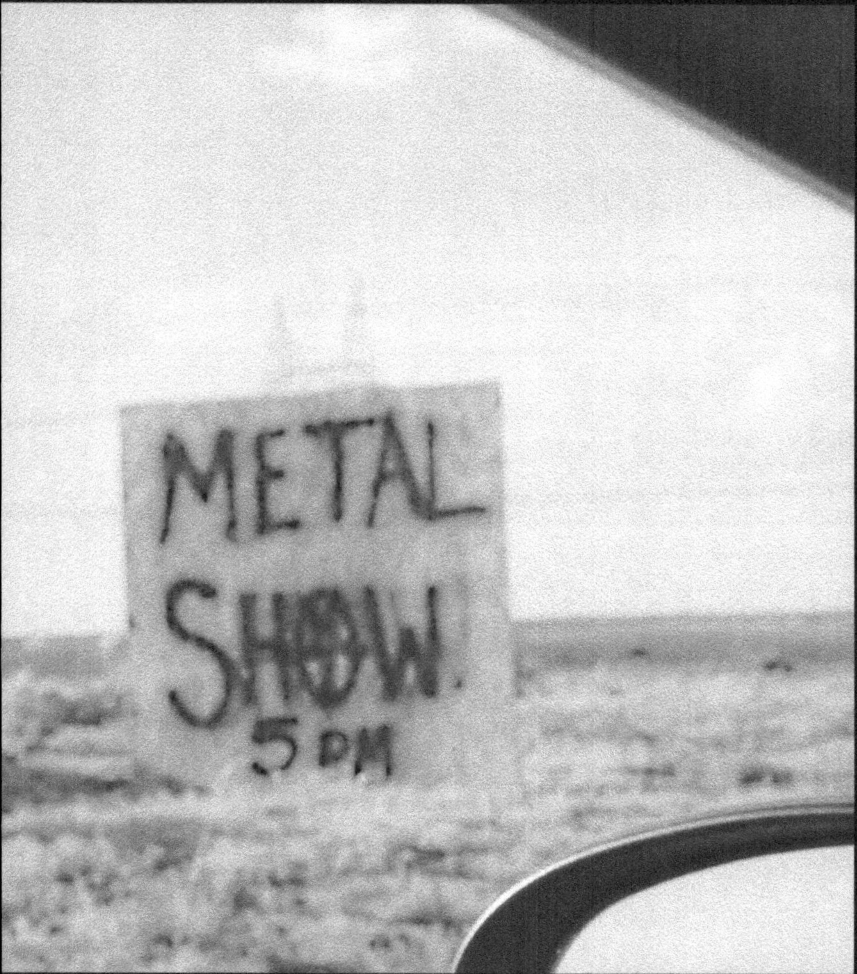
METAL
SHOW.
5 PM

**23 & 24.** Testify

# 3 The Band

At the heart of rez metal, the bands strum their fiery chords and scream their powerful lyrics. Within the cacophonous rez metal scene, a few bands have garnered attention beyond Indian Country, attracting the likes of luminaries such as Metallica producer Flemming Rasmussen. This chapter zooms into the rhythms of these bands, focusing on their origins and on the stories of I Don't Konform, Testify, and Signal 99. These bands shatter generational boundaries, mixing old with new, parents with their kids, "urban" Indians with rural towns, tradition with innovation. As with heavy metal bands emerging around the world, rez metal defies the usual conventions.

## Testify

■ "I would play at the sheep corral."

The band Testify started about five years ago. And first it was just me and my dad. Then we went through a few lineup changes and we found David Sebastian. He stepped up, writing the music and joining the band. And he kind of found the true sound of what Testify was. The reason we picked the name Testify was to make a statement of our music. And to put it out there. Without speaking with our music. Pretty much testifying. We're testifying about our—how to deal with situations. And that's how we get with our music. We don't resort to violence or drugs or anything like that. It's more how to overcome lifestyle situations that you don't

**25.** Testify

know how to deal with. And for us, the way we deal with our problems is through music. We let the music do the speaking through the emotions that we have.

I joined the band in January 2013. I was a good friend of Edmund [Yazzie] since my midteens. So when he asked me if I wanted to join the band as a bassist, I just thought maybe I could feel him out. Check out the bass. I've been playing music since I was in high school freshman year. And it's been a real inspiration to me because it's helped me cope with things. Especially with the situation that I went through. So it's a stress reliever. That's like the basic history. I used to live in Albuquerque, and on some weekends I would come back home, and I would just head to David's place and just ask anyone who would give me guitar lessons. And this one visit he asked me if I wanted to join them as a tour player. So we talked about it and I basically moved back from Albuquerque, back home, and joined the band circuit. And

I've now been playing the guitar since I was sixteen. Music for me is something that I can always count on. Then, at the end of the day, or whenever I'm feeling down or anything, I can just put on my earphones and listen to music. That's how I joined the band Testify.

[Earlier I had] started off with drums. I would play at the sheep corral that we used to have at Crown Point, and then I'd grab a couple of sticks and start beating on fifty-five-gallon drums that we used to feed our livestock. And I noticed that the rhythm was there and I had an interest in percussion. I started off asking my dad if I could get a kit. No drum lessons until I got to high school. And it just all fell into place as far as my drumming. I played in the high school band. I played in a lot of country bands, which didn't really go [anywhere]. But it was a way to get some exposure. I was actually hired, and my first gig I remember playing at a club at the Sleekly because I was under age and in Gallup, and I got paid thirty dollars. And to me that was a lot of money at the time. And then I went to the county police academy and became an officer, and ever since then I thought I didn't have time for drama anymore. And so I stopped playing for a while.

[Then a couple of guys found out I played] drums, and they asked if I could come over and play them. And we went to this hogan, where they had all their equipment. The song we played was Metallica and then a cover song. And then Ozzy. I thought: this is pretty cool. So that's where I started kicking, and I always had the love for metal music even when playing in country music. We started a band called Double Edge with a kid from Marianna Lake who just had a super talent. It was a two-man show, but we were starting to get noticed and actually were set up to have a tour in Russia. We were gonna get paid and we were working on our passports. But there were some personal issues that came up. There really hasn't been a Native band that actually performed in Russia. We got pretty well known.

We've come a long way. I'm really fortunate. You know the boys will do their thing. We are blessed with a six-year-old daughter, Caylee, and that's our family time. And so I'm really pleased to see where we're at with the music because it's my passion. I'm an elected official—third term—on the Navajo Nation Council. And I tell my people that there's a venue that pays me to support my family. To play music. We get people who come up to us and say, "You know I really like this song because it relates to how I am—how I feel, and I didn't have the answer before but now I do." So here's something that really makes the whole work process worth it. All the troubles that we go through as a band, all the financial issues that we have, and all the little things that happened—hearing people say that we made a difference in their life is what makes this whole thing worth it. That's all that matters.

We have a few people who don't agree with what we do. But we're not there to pick a fight. We're not there to bash them. We do what we do for a reason, and some people get it. Some people don't. For those who don't get it, maybe they will one day, or maybe they won't. We try to reach out to everyone, but of course we can't make everyone happy. We can't reach out to every single person. Some people relate to other things. We're all different. But for those who connect to the music, who connect to metal, we're all a big family whether we're a band or whether we're a fan at a show. Either way it's all about family. So we look out for each other, and that's what we do.

Some of our most memorable moments: our past gig in Zuni. A fan, I recall, was standing on the side of the stage when I was performing. He just kept watching me the whole time. He had a little boy with him. I guess it was his son. But after the show was done they both came up to me, and they were telling me, "Like wow, you're really great." You know that's a really rewarding feeling, to know that you made a difference in their lives and that you made a deep impact on them. That's the number one moment. It's just a great feeling.

One of the memorable moments for me was when we got a chance to open up for Mushroomhead this past April. Back in high school they were one of my top five bands I listened to. So once we got the news that we would get to open up for them, it was pretty much a dream come true. And I told my friends, "Don't give up on whatever you're trying to do." Just keep it up and don't give up. And that's the main point. Just don't give up on your dreams, 'cause it will happen. Wherever challenges come out, you just keep your head up and shoot for the stars.

Lyrically the music is more about past experiences we went through. For example, our song "Rage" talks about kind of fighting with the inner self. You want to do something but then the other part of you doesn't want to do it. So it's more like a clash of how to deal. We also have another song about our Navajo Code Talkers, for our veterans too, which is called "Codes of Honor." And that recognizes all the trauma that these veterans went through when they went to war. And how hard it was. And how difficult it was. We've had veterans in the family. So we know. We've heard what they said. And we put it into song. Guitarwise, David will bring his melodies, his riffs, and we'll just take it step by step. And the way I describe it, it's like making a cake. You start with your foundation and you just add more things. The more stuff you add, the better it gets. And we can't do it as well with one person. It takes all four of us actually to make a song. So it's a starting process, but we have fun with it too. That's the main thing.

Heavy metal is a source of feelings that in some weird way grants you energy. And when you're stressed, when you're mad, you hear that guitar match with the kick drum, or you hear the vocals, or this certain lyric describes exactly how you feel. And you feel that connection, and that relieves some type of stress, some type of tension.

That's how it works for me. Some dark, dark, dark past issues that can be connected to the issues that the young people are facing. We talk about some of these issues. One of the songs that I wrote is called "Beneath the Ashes." The lyrics are about moving on from a dark phase of chaos in your life. We all go through bumps in life and some are the deeper ones. It's kind of hard to get past those issues. In one case of suicide, Rue was a good friend of mine. It was a tough time for me once I heard the news. So I pretty much just wrote all my feelings down in a notebook and I turned those little short stories into lyrics. And that's how "Beneath the Ashes" came about.

Kids from the reservation are facing suicide as a number one problem; a couple of years ago there was a rash of suicides happening, five or ten suicides within that period. One of the victims was a relative of mine. That was really devastating to the family. To this day you know there is still trauma from that. And I believe the whole reservation has that same issue. Another issue is poverty. It's all over the reservation. There's the jobless rate. There is the unemployment rate of over 50 percent, I believe. It's pretty high. People don't really don't have an income. Every family on the reservation deals with that. Poverty. Another critical issue is domestic violence. I've had past experiences with that, with close family members and that's not a pretty situation at all. You always hear that in the newspapers and over the reservation. It's just kind of sad to hear that. It goes on all the time. With the music, with our music, we try to write about stuff like that.

With the youth, the main problem is alcohol. And the parents not being parents. The kids not knowing where parents are. And when the kids have siblings, it's up to them to take care of [the younger ones]. And for them I see that it's very frustrating for them. Because they want

**26.** I Don't Konform

to be kids, to go out with their friends. They want to go to the movies, but instead they have to fulfill that role of being a parent at a young age. Alcohol is really on the rise and taking a lot of lives—destroying a lot of things, and I think that's pretty much the reason for all the problems that we have here. And we try to tell the kids: don't find your resources in alcohol. Find sport and music. Something else. There's a lot of smart kids around here. We want the kids to have the right mindset. So it's a work in progress for us. As long as we're getting the message out, that's all that matters.

## I Don't Konform and Flemming Rasmussen

■ "The tribal vice president is really a headbanger."

RASMUSSEN. Three Native dudes from the west! Pretty early on in my career, I decided not to move to the States. So I'm mainly doing local

**27.** I Don't Konform

Danish bands, and I'm doing the odd international act on and off. And when I was contacted on the whole project [debut album for I Don't Konform, IDK], I thought: interesting. I think the whole idea of Natives and the reservation and all this kind of caught me up. I heard the music and I really liked it. It's got, you know, that aggression that I haven't heard in while. So I got really interested in IDK. And we started talking and we got it working.

CECIL. We were recently in the *Navajo Times* as well. Yeah, we've been bugging a lot of people since this started. And obviously we have to fundraise. We've been fundraising for about six months now. We've been harassing a lot of people. *Navajo Times*—we bugged them. President's office—we bugged them, to get the word out there to help us fundraise. And you know it paid off.

We'll be hitting the road tomorrow. We leave Friday morning for Copenhagen, Denmark. Which is where we're recording. So [don't] forget we have never really been out of the reservation. Not on a plane. You know that's how crazy I am. First we fly from Denver to Chicago and Chicago to Waldorf, Germany. Board a train. And then from there we catch a high speed train to Copenhagen. We were all just in shock. The second night Flemming was here, our drummer Randy Bailey too—we were all sitting around. We took Flemming to one of our family spots on top of the hill and we were just taking it in, like, "Wow, wow!" We asked, "What do you think about our reservation? It's your first time here." "It's very different from what I imagined. I didn't really know what to expect. It's definitely not as green as I expected."

RASMUSSEN. Well there's a lot of shit I don't know, but I must admit I really enjoy it. It's pulling me more thanks to the people that I'm meeting with than to the actual spot. I'm not sure it will be my number one on my list of favorite places to move. I flew out here for preproduction. So we've been working on songs and we actually practiced in a hogan and in Window Rock.

CECIL. Right now we're focusing on just doing the album. That's the main goal—having a good sounding album that we want to hear, and then we're going to be looking for labels to release it. There should be several labels interested, but you never know about these things. Yeah, that's the plan. This is an opportunity; there are no guarantees.

KYLE FELTER. One thing I want to say—I want to thank the offices of our tribal president and vice president. They have been more than supportive and helpful for our band, and this would not have happened five years ago, definitely not ten years ago. There's been a shift in consciousness about heavy metal music among our tribal leaders, and it's positive, and we're really digging it right now. Also the vice president is really a headbanger.

**28–30.** Signal 99

## Signal 99

■ "The good thing is the crowds really get into it."

The metal scene on the reservation is thriving. You've got your different genres. And a lot of it's hard. I enjoy it because you get people. From all across the different areas you can see the influences. From one spot to another you can just see it really is a community of musicians who share the same interests. That's what I like about the area. You know, we're not like a big metro area where bands are all from one section. Although we're all from the same geographic zone, it's a big region and you can see all the different influences. So we kind of have our own scene going in this area. I think it's pretty cool, the metal that's coming from New Mexico in particular. Considering the area, there's a lot of anger. You'll see the unemployment, you'll see the poverty, and this is our world. This is our little bubble of political disenfranchisement, and you can see it coming out through the music. You can see the anger coming out. You can hear the lyrics. You can see the people you interact with. It's a very rhythmic music. I've noticed that most of the metal here is rhythmic.

Compared to when you go and play in Denver or Tucson, when you're playing out here in the rural areas or in the urban areas that are within a reservation area, most of the music is very rhythmic, and the good thing is the crowds really get into it. The crowd participation and the metal scene here are quite amazing. Big crowds. Enthusiastic crowds. People come out and share a common bond where everyone's going through the same thing—we can all connect. We can all relate to a lot of these issues. So when you come out there, it's like family. That's the reason why you get a lot of these people coming out to support each other, because we all know what we're going through. And we start establishing relationships with other people. That's the best way I can explain why some of these shows are actually pretty big. Because we all can relate to everything that's going on. That's just it. My family. I think sometimes people just want to rock the fuck out. Forget about the bad that's going on and everything else like that. This is an act, and you give yourself a damn headache and a neck ache just banging a head for a night—just for good.

Heavy metal has a bad reputation of leading to suicide and self-destruction, etc. Different people come off as aggressive. It goes back to something that's different than what people are used to. They attach a negative feeling or emotion to it. So I think that's why people have this thing against metal music, but really it's about emotions; poetry is really what it is. Poetry from the dark side of metal, and we're just expressing ourselves. There's nothing wrong with feeling angry. There's nothing wrong with feeling depressed. There's nothing wrong with feeling how you won or lost, and you just put it down. Just put it into something that you can actually hear, and people enjoy it.

People can connect with that. Being in a band is so that we can bring all these issues and then share with everyone else. If we can share with everyone else—if we can reach out to somebody and show them, "Hey, you know life can't really be that bad"—it really just takes all the energy and applies it to something else something that's more productive.

Teen suicide is a huge issue here. I was talking to the vice president, and he really thinks that this kind metal festival pretty much helps people to cope with it. It's something we can all relate to. We all know somebody who's taken their life. We probably all have one member of our families who did take their life. I think a lot of people who have suicidal thoughts don't understand that. It's a very internal battle. Depression is a very individual battle that people go through. Any form or any way that you can allow a person to have expression and to express their hate or their sadness or their anger or their pain, then you're giving them a way to cope with that in an external way instead of an internal way. I think that's a good thing. I think all music serves that purpose. I think heavy metal in itself doesn't shy away from the pain. It doesn't shy away. From the blood, the gore, the damage, the carnage. It puts it in your face, and I think that's a good thing and I think that's inspiring. People can go and they can express themselves. They can shake their fist in the air. They can scream. They can cry. That's a lot better than doing it by yourself and thinking about a gun.

It's like, when I'm feeling down I go and play my guitar. There are different emotions. And, I believe, different songs—you'll feel anger, you'll feel sadness, or feel happiness. It's just an outlet for me to cope with it. That's how I cope with losing family members. It's always going to be there for me, and it's something that I enjoy doing too as well.

I think music's real big art around here. When you go to a show you see it firsthand yourself. You see everybody there enjoying time with each other and having fun. Forgetting about the real world out there that you have to go back to. I think having little places like the little venues we have here is good. Just people like my brother right here. You know music helps people like that. Cope with it that way, you know, through music, and that's pretty much it for me.

I think it's always been popular. It's true. I think it's always been there. It's just that sometimes the music was not really at the venues. Like when we first started, I was always booking places at nontraditional venues. So that's why when you go out to the rez, there are a lot of nontraditional venues out there meeting people. They pick a spot. They find a place to play. And that's the scene. There are not really a lot of places to play. Like we couldn't just go down the street, book a show, and play. So the other two alternatives were to have either house shows or backyard shows—you know, book a park or whatever. You don't just get together, and that's one of the reasons why [Country Alibi] opens because, you know, it's his garage.

So it's just people creating their own places to play. That's really what the scene is, like, about in this area. A scene has always been there. It's just that you know you have to go and find places. That's kind of cool because it's like an underground. I think some people are finally seeing some of these parts of it, because I think a lot of it has to do with social media. Because everyone has access to social media, and now you can hear that there's a show going on here, or you can just share more openly.

Before social media became dominant you wrote out flyers wherever, trying to find these dudes. But now it's like everyone has information, and you can find these things now. So it makes it huge. But really in reality it's always been there; it's just that social media has really exposed the local music scene, which has always been your festivals, your fairs, getting on a stage at the fair, etc. So that would happen in any rural area. If you could get on the Shiprock fair stage, or you got on the fair stage in Tuba City, then you accomplished something. There are many things that I think help control alcohol besides law enforcement around here trying to stop it.

Half of these bands don't even know how to play the big stages, more often than not. They don't get their opportunities. It was nice to see a lot more coming into this area now—more movies and stuff. The New Mexico stuff. And, we realized, we were hoping that the metal scene would explode with that, but it really didn't. It kind of declined. So everywhere else opened up. Arizona, Colorado, places like that have been home for us, and it's been great. But we just want to see more out of the area. You know there's a lot that can be helped if people just take the chance and do it very well. I don't really know Rasmussen, but I would think there's probably just a story of three Natives looking to break out, and then I think that's like a lot of our dreams. You know when we first start music, it's to make it big. Growing up as little kids, a lot of us dreamed of playing the big stage, playing in front of hundreds of people. But the reality of it is, to be successful it's totally work. It's not just talent, it's work.

These dreams of trying to make it big—it's a different era now. It's not like it used to be twenty years ago. Now it's like everything is so chaotic. You have to do it on your own. These days you can't rely on playing one big gig or one time just to get one record deal. We'll just give you like a million dollars advance, or something like that. I understand it's like we're all taking chances. Rolling the dice. Hoping to get that one moment of either recognition or success of fifteen minutes of fame and it's your one hit song. A lot of bands respect that, because we're all struggling to make ends meet. The goal is to become a full-time musician, to make a living off it. So you have to take those chances, and that's probably why Rasmussen saw that they're rolling the dice—let's give them a chance to see. Let's see if they can do it.

When I started the music, I didn't really sing about the issues. I did my writing as a whole person, as a human being. You could relate to anybody, regardless of race or what reservation you're from, or anything like that. So when I started going out I was playing all these different areas. We have such a huge fan base now that it's not strictly Native Americans. It's across the board. Now they're seeing us as a band and not a reservation band. I think to be successful in this area, we have to start removing certain labels and just focus on the music. I think that probably has something to do with the success of the band. When I first saw Signal 99 back in the day, one of the things that struck me was that their presentation of their music was lively. Their music was groovy, and it was a lot different than any other local band that was playing that type of sound or music. Their level of performance was "big city." Here in Farmington, it just always struck me as: "Wow, you know these guys really have it."

When I got the opportunity to work, I knew from the very beginning: "This is a band that at least I'm not going have to worry about. We're going play in Austin. We're going to go play in Denver. We're going to go play in Phoenix. We get out." And he takes the music to the next level. It's just a matter of exposure really. I mean even out here in the Southwest it's still a small market. This isn't London. This isn't New York. And it's a matter of getting this talent in front of the people who pay for it. And that's really what this is—exposure. And not only does Signal 99 have it—there are other bands who have the talent but will not drive to these cities. I really appreciate you [Signal 99] coming out here and putting this out there. Hopefully that will bear the fruit that it needs to.

**31.** Rez Metal house parties

My advice to some of the local bands, to the bands who are struggling, is: If you want big, think big and always keep it at that level. Don't worry about anything else, because if you're out there doing something that you believe in and you're actually putting in that effort, and you're showing that, somebody is going to grab a hold of it. So just do your thing. Just keep it as real as you can. I love you guys, you know, just true to themselves. If you want something big and go for it, there's no no. Way to go. No looking back. I mean, it may be a big risk, but take off from there. People are going to talk—people always talk. But stay true to yourself, and just keep going—you know things are possible.

We share all share the same emotions and human emotions. We're just people fighting the same fight as you are every day. We just get to do it in a much more beautiful place. We all know that feeling of when you first record your song, and you first put it on something physical you can hold. It is a strange concept, because you hear music; you

**32.** Rez Metal house parties

hear it. But to put it in [a format] you can actually hold and show and share with somebody else—it's a very emotional time when you do your first recording, when you do your first thing, and say, "Look. All this hard work. I can actually hold it now. I can actually share it with somebody physically." It's like a big circle, isn't it? Especially around here. This is a real small community. In the metal scene, you see all the same faces. We go to each other's concerts. It's really good. It's a really good thing. I don't see that in the bigger cities really.

So right now we're in the process of editing. And it is a lot of work. Either we go and pay someone thousands of dollars which we don't have, or we do it ourselves. And the cool thing about doing it ourselves is that we learn from doing it. We all share the same fans. We're all family. And that's how I treat them. I want to show you can do whatever you want if you're successful at it and then go do it and work hard. Yeah, work hard, and one of the things I want to show, not only to my son but to everyone else is that if you work hard, you'll get results. They might not be the results you're looking, for but you never know who's watching you. You might have another little kid watching you and saying, "Hey, you know these guys are pretty cool." And we hope the next person, the next generation, can take it to the next level after that. Just to hear if we have that kind of influence—I don't see us as role models, but young people do see role models, and they genuinely inspire people. Then I think that makes it worth it. It's worth more than money. You can't put a price to that and that's worth so much more.

**33.** Melanie Nez

# 4 Industry, Audience, and the Next Generation

It remains to consider the fans and the future of rez metal, which promises more innovation. From groupies to deejays to music teachers, Navajos young and old have come to embrace the transformative nature of rez metal. Women have increasingly asserted themselves into the scene, and the rez metal community has embraced their creativity. Even more impactfully, Navajo high schools have begun to incorporate rez metal into their curriculum, providing guitar instruction through organizations like the Native American Music Fund. This chapter also looks at the effects of heavy metal beyond the usual venues and in other Native communities, including Hopi and Zuni.

## Melanie Nez

■ "I was really scared until I started jamming."

I grew up with my dad and he was the first person who inspired me to start playing guitar. So I kinda liked jamming metal tunes on his guitar and in his space. That's how I got into the metal. But also when I first started playing guitar, when I was young, I really wanted to play like Waylon Jennings and Johnny Cash because I could hang out with my dad and jam some old country tunes. And then I went into the garage with my uncle and listened to Metallica and Anthrax. I got into that music.

The very first metal song I learned on guitar was "Seek and Destroy" by Metallica. My uncle brought me a Metallica tattoo. Yeah. He saw me playing acoustic and he took me to the guitar shop. He was like, "Go pick out a guitar," and I went to go pick up an acoustic. I wanted to play country, but he was like, "Put that back," and he gave me an electric instead. That was ten years ago. I went to a Christian school that had this really awesome music teacher. She taught me how to read notes. And from there I just started playing. I just really like older music. For me, my earliest band I remember is probably ACDC. And as a young kid [I knew] quite a few kids who listened to heavy metal. I would hang out with my friends, and then I had some friends who would listen to country music also. So yeah, I was kind of inspired by country and heavy metal, and it was really nice.

The first time I played in front of people, Kyle (from I Don't Konform) told me to come and play and I was really shy. I think at the time the only people I knew there were Kyle and the drummer. I didn't really talk to them; I didn't talk to anyone. I was really scared until I started jamming. I remember when I started playing I saw everyone heading and singing along. And that's when I felt comfortable. People were just having fun. When you see people just enjoying themselves and enjoying the music that you're playing, it makes you feel comfortable and happy.

## Condemn the World

■ "Metal is also about heartbreak."

Nature's all around us and kind of helps with the writing process of new music, and we're hearing new stuff coming from everybody. When I grew up it was nothing but music around, so I was inspired by music, my dad's music. But I wanted to play something a little different. So my

**34.** Condemn the World

dad got me my first drum set when I was six. I have been working since then. Most people think that country is all about love and inspiration. But metal is also about heartbreak. If you look closely at the lyrics, they're really meaningful—a message to people, like "never give up," and "just keep going with the flow." That's what our lyrics are mainly about. One of the songs, a slow one, was written from an experience that we had in the past two years dealing with suicide in our family and having the last two cousins die within two years of each other. It really grows [overwhelming] and you start to miss that person. It's a sticky issue here. It seems that it's happening in high school. It bothered me to think that some kids would just throw their life away for someone who didn't love them, when someone out there really can love them. It bothered me a lot because of course you're losing a life.

And also they have parents, who are probably still heartbroken to this day. I mean, I would never do that to my parents. And I now

**35.** Kimberly Berchman

know how that felt because I lost two cousins the same way. It was a really hard song to write because I had so much feeling in there and so many emotions. It was meant to touch other people as well, to let them know that suicide is not the way out. There is a way you can conquer this feeling inside.

## Kimberly Berchman, Owner of Navajo Metal Promotions

■ "Navajo origin stories have always spoken to musicians."

My name is Kimberly Berchman. I am the owner of Navajo Metal Promotions. It's an independent music page where we can all communicate. It's used in order to support all bands.

There's no negativity. We don't allow any of that. All the bands can give us all the information that they want shared, whether they need a new member, whether they have an upcoming show—whatever they need to share. Navajo Metal Promotions also exists to connect all the pieces of the metal scene of the entire nation and surrounding tribes. We have the eastern agency and the western agency. We have the Zuni tribe. We have Laguna. We have people from Albuquerque. They all come together. This entire scene is all going to be "we're all in it together." The metal scene is a complete brotherhood. You'll see half of the audience of the show is a member of another band. Metal has become one of the main forms of expression for Navajos. Our grandparents experienced all this oppression. Our parents experienced some form of oppression, especially with boarding schools. And we are the first generation to have to deal with that. I believe we have all this anger and aggression toward everything that we've been put through.

Yet we're still here. We're here to try. We're here to express ourselves. Navajo origin stories have always spoken to musicians. We've always been artists. We've had drama since the beginning. We've been singers of origin stories, which involves singing prayers. A lot of these bands continue that tradition of singing or playing music. It's in our blood. It says the people we grew up from were created from the sand, from there with the help of our deities and their prayers their songs. We're able to be here today. And I think metal is kind of like the modern version of what our ancestors had been doing for centuries. Gathering together, meeting together. This is our way of gathering together. The first metal shows popped up in the middle of nowhere and still they're getting the crowd. We have brothers here supporting each other's families. Grandparents, grandchildren—they're all here in the music scene.

I think some of the obstacles that we're facing come from outside perceptions. People think it's all negative. They think we're here getting drunk, here doing drugs—but we're not. Everyone here is sober, just

**36.** Jeff Lee

performing, expressing ourselves. There is a problem with illicit drug use, with suicide rates, with everything. And there is anger from our generation. And this is a way to express it: we're here. We all know what metal is. We all know it's a positive thing in our lives, and we want to continue it. That's why we keep going to shows even though we have to drive hours and hours. We're still here to support everybody supporting each other.

## Jeff Lee, Teen Music Program

■ "There's probably more bands here than you'll find in a big city."

My name is Jeff. I'm from here. I play with the band Muddy Souls and we are here for the teens, for a music program that basically involves dealing with the teens who are at risk. We try to point them in the right direction musically. It's really important for them to have some kind of experience of music for their own well-being, their own knowledge, to take them out into the world to experience more things. I believe it's proper to give back to our community and help the kids. A lot of the students here are at risk. All teens on the Navajo Reservation are at risk to drugs and alcohol. It's an everyday thing here, and music is the only way we know that we can have them in a safe environment which expresses the positiveness of music. It just helps their overall confidence in themselves, in life, in general.

I grew up on the reservation and I've lived all over the United States. But to me this is home. I love the area. I'm from the reservation and this is my home. The most popular genres, I believe, would be country music and heavy metal. Those are two extremes, and they're so extreme. There's no in between. We try to fill that gap by playing the blues. But music is music. I believe however you express yourself—whether it be country, the blues, Spanish music, heavy metal, thrash—it's all music, sound, and vibrations. That's the gist of it. As far as I'm concerned, why pop music is so popular is because it's out there in the media. And on any given weekend you can go anywhere and you'll find country bands playing somewhere in practically every community. I say it's either heavy metal or country. There's no in between.

I think heavy metal music is a lot bigger on the reservation than it is off. I hear so many bands. Music is one thing that you do see in this community. There are probably more bands here than you'll find in a big city, mainly because, you know, there's nothing else to do.

We try to bring the students up, get them on stage, have them express themselves, play music, and go from there. Just seeing them progress musically—that's the biggest satisfaction.

**37–40.** Teen workshop, Native American Music Fund

# NOTES

### 1. WHAT IS REZ METAL?

1. The El Rancho hotel, in fact, lures in I-40 travelers to explore the glamour of the "Old West" of the 1930s–1940s.
2. See Amundson, *Yellowcake Towns*.
3. See Jacobsen, *Sound of Navajo Country*, discussed further later.
4. Jacobsen, *Sound of Navajo Country*, 1.
5. For an excellent overview of these scenes, see Berlund et al., *Indigenous Pop*. Also see Wright-McLeod, *Encyclopedia of Native Music*.
6. The provenance of "rez metal" is not clear, but the genre reaches back into the 1990s. See Turkewitz, "Looking to Uplift."
7. For marching bands and the intersection of boarding schools, colonialism, and cultural appropriation, see Deloria, *Indians in Unexpected Places*, 183–223; Troutman, *Indian Blues*; also see Geiogamah and Darby, *American Indian Performing Arts*.
8. Recent scholarship has explored every aspect of Indigenous music. See Berlund et al., *Indigenous Pop*; Wright-McLeod, *Encyclopedia of Native Music*. For the expansion of drum music and powwow culture, see Harris, *Heartbeat, Warble*; Browner, *Music of the First Nations*. For the ethnographic history of recording Indigenous music, see Levine, *Writing American Indian Music*; and Patterson, *Natalie Curtis Burlin*. For exporting the steel guitar, see Troutman, *Kika Kila*.
9. For an overview of the changing nature and study of "world music," see Johnson, "A Critical Discourse Analysis of World Music"; also see Nooshin, "Introduction to the Special Issue."
10. For a comprehensive overview of recent trends in contemporary American Indian art, see Rosenthal, "Rewriting the Narrative."
11. The scholarship on contemporary Indian art is vast. Some recent overviews include Hill, *Creativity Is Our Tradition*; Hillaire, *A Totem Pole History*; Horton, *Art*

*for an Undivided Earth*; Lentis, *Colonized through Art*; Passalucqua and Morris, *Native Art Now!*; Siebert, *Indian Playing Indian*; and Snyder, *John Joseph Mathews*.

12. Sherman and Dooley, *The Sioux Chef's Indigenous Kitchen*.
13. For an examination of the Cold War West, see Montoya, "Landscapes of the Cold War West."
14. Numerous studies have explored the boom-and-bust cycles of uranium mining in the West, several of which I cite later. Some of the more recent include Ringholz, *Uranium Frenzy*, and Amundson, *Yellowcake Towns*. For an overview of the shifts in Navajo economic strategies before this period, see White, *Roots of Dependency*.
15. Iverson, *Navajo Nation*, 130.
16. Grinde and Johansen, *Ecocide of Native America*, 205.
17. For Anna Rondon quote, see Eichstaedt, *If You Poison Us*, 47, quoting Anna Rondon, personal communication, November 1992. For Joe Shirley quote, see "Navajos Mark 30th Anniversary of Spill," *News from Indian Country*, July 2009.
18. See Voyles, *Wastelanding*; also see Pasternak, *Yellow Dirt*.
19. See Mays, *Hip Hop Beats, Indigenous Rhymes*.
20. For recent work on the benefits of metal and other forms of extreme music, see Sharman and Dingle, "Extreme Metal Music and Anger Processing."
21. Heavy metal scholarship (known as "metal studies") has steadily increased as the genre goes global. For classic texts, see Gaines, *Teenage Wasteland*; Hjelm et al., *Heavy Metal*; Pillsbury, *Damage Incorporated*; Wallach et al., *Metal Rules the Globe*; Walser, *Running with the Devil*; Weinstein, *Heavy Metal: A Cultural Sociology*; Weinstein, *Heavy Metal: The Music and Its Subculture*.
22. Wallach et al., *Metal Rules the Globe*, 8.

www.ingramcontent.com/pod-product-compliance
Lightning Source LLC
LaVergne TN
LVHW040619250326
834688LV00035B/638

## SOURCES AND FURTHER READING

Amundson, Michael. *Yellowcake Towns: Uranium Mining Communities in the American West.* Boulder: University of Colorado Press, 2002.

Berlund, Jeff, Jan Johnson, and Kimerli Lee. *Indigenous Pop: Native American Music from Jazz to Hip Hop.* Tucson: University of Arizona Press, 2016.

Browner, Tara, ed. *Music of the First Nations: Tradition and Innovation in Native North America.* Urbana: University of Illinois Press, 2010.

Deloria, Philip J. *Indians in Unexpected Places.* Norman: University of Oklahoma Press, 2004.

Eichstaedt, Peter H. *If You Poison Us: Uranium and Native Americans.* Santa Fe NM: Red Crane Books, 1994.

Gaines, Donna. *Teenage Wasteland: Suburbia's Dead End Kids.* Chicago: University of Chicago Press, [1998] 1990.

Geiogamah, Hanay, and Jaye T. Darby, eds. *American Indian Performing Arts: Critical Directions.* Los Angeles: UCLA American Indian Studies Center, 2009.

Grinde, Donald A., and Bruce E. Johansen. *Ecocide of Native America: Environmental Destruction of Indian Lands and Peoples.* Santa Fe NM: Clear Light Publishers, 1995.

Harris, Craig. *Heartbeat, Warble, and the Electric Powwow: American Indian Music.* Norman: University of Oklahoma Press, 2016.

Hill, Richard. *Creativity Is Our Tradition: Three Decades of Contemporary Indian Art at the Institute of American Indian Arts.* Santa Fe NM: Institute of American Indian Art, 1992.

Hillaire, Pauline. *A Totem Pole History: The Work of Lummi Carver Joe Hillaire.* Edited by Gregory Fields. Lincoln: University of Nebraska Press, 2013.

Hjelm, Titus, Keith Kahn-Harris, and Mark LeVine, eds. *Heavy Metal: Controversies and Countercultures.* Sheffield, UK: Equinox Publishing, 2013.

Horton, Jessica. *Art for an Undivided Earth: The American Indian Movement Generation.* Durham NC: Duke University Press, 2017.

Iverson, Peter. *The Navajo Nation.* Westport CT: Greenwood Press, 1981.

Jacobsen, Kristina. *The Sound of Navajo Country: Music, Language, and Diné Belonging.* Albuquerque: University of New Mexico Press, 2017.

Johnson, Kathy. "A Critical Discourse Analysis of World Music as the 'Other' in Education." *Research in Music Education* 19, no. 1 (2002): 14–21.

Lentis, Marinella. *Colonized through Art: American Indian Schools and Art Education, 1889–1919.* Lincoln: University of Nebraska Press, 2017

Levine, Victoria Lindsay. *Writing American Indian Music: Historic Transcriptions, Notations, and Arrangements.* Middleton WI: American Musicological Society, 2002.

Mays, Kyle. *Hip Hop Beats, Indigenous Rhymes: Modernity and Hip Hop in Indigenous North America.* Albany NY: SUNY Press, 2018.

Montoya, Maria E. "Landscapes of the Cold War West." In *Cold War American West, 1945–1989,* ed. Kevin J. Fernlund, 9–27. Albuquerque: University of New Mexico Press, 1998.

Nooshin, Lauden. "Introduction to the Special Issue: The Ethnomusicology of Western Art Music." *Ethnomusicology Forum* 20, no. 3 (December 2011): 285–300.

Passalucqua, Veronica, and Kate Morris, eds. *Native Art Now!: Developments in Contemporary Native American Art Since 1992.* Indianapolis IN: Eiteljorg Museum of American Indians and Western Art, 2017.

Pasternak, Judy. *Yellow Dirt: A Poisoned Land and the Betrayal of the Navajos.* New York: Free Press, 2011.

Patterson, Michelle Wick. *Natalie Curtis Burlin: A Life in Native and African American Music.* Lincoln: University of Nebraska Press, 2010.

Pillsbury, Glenn T. *Damage Incorporated: Metallica and the Production of Musical Identity.* New York: Routledge Press, 2006.

Ringholz, Raye C. *Uranium Frenzy: Saga of the Nuclear West.* Logan: Utah State University, 2002.

Rosenthal, Nick. "Rewriting the Narrative: American Indian Artists in California, 1960s–1980s." *Western Historical Quarterly* 49 (Winter 2018): 409–36.

Sharman, Leah, and Genevieve A. Dingle. "Extreme Metal Music and Anger Processing." *Frontiers in Human Neuroscience* 9 (May 2015).

Sherman, Sean, with Beth Dooley. *The Sioux Chef's Indigenous Kitchen.* Minneapolis: University of Minnesota Press, 2017.

Siebert, Monika. *Indian Playing Indian: Multiculturalism and Contemporary Indigenous Art in North America.* Tuscaloosa: University of Alabama Press, 2015.

Snyder, Michael. *John Joseph Mathews: Life of an Osage Writer.* Norman: University of Oklahoma Press, 2017.

Troutman, John W. *Indian Blues: American Indians and the Politics of Music, 1879–1934.* Norman: University of Oklahoma Press, 2009.

——— . *Kika Kila: How the Hawaiian Steel Guitar Changed the Sound of Modern Music.* Chapel Hill: University of North Carolina Press, 2016.

Turkewitz, Julie. "Looking to Uplift, with Navajo 'Rez Metal.'" *New York Times*, January 25, 2015.

Voyles, Traci. *Wastelanding: Legacies of Uranium Mining in Navajo Country.* Minneapolis: University of Minnesota Press, 2015.

Wallach, Jeremy, Harris M. Berger, and Paul D. Greene, eds. *Metal Rules the Globe.* Durham NC: Duke University Press, 2011.

Walser, Robert. *Running with the Devil: Power, Gender, and Madness in Heavy Metal Music.* Middleton CT: Wesleyan University Press, 1993.

Weinstein, Deena. *Heavy Metal: A Cultural Sociology.* New York: Lexington Books, 1991.

——— . *Heavy Metal: The Music and Its Subculture.* New York: Da Capo Press, 2000.

White, Richard. *The Roots of Dependency: Subsistence, Environment, and Social Change among the Choctaws, Pawnees, and Navajos.* Lincoln: University of Nebraska Press, 1983.

Wright-McLeod, Brian. *The Encyclopedia of Native Music: More than a Century of Recordings from Wax Cylinder to the Internet.* Tucson: University of Arizona Press, 2005.